Invasive Exotic Plant Monitoring (Year 2) and Treatment Recommendations for Lincoln Boyhood National Memorial

Natural Resource Report Series NPS/HTLN/NRR—2012/569

Craig C. Young, Jordan C. Bell, Chad S. Gross, and Ashley D. Dunkle

National Park Service, Heartland I&M Network
Wilson's Creek National Battlefield
6424 West Farm Road 182
Republic, MO 64738

Heartland Network
Natural Resource Monitoring

The National Park Service, Natural Resource Stewardship and Science office in Fort Collins, Colorado publishes a range of reports that address natural resource topics of interest and applicability to a broad audience in the National Park Service and others in natural resource management, including scientists, conservation and environmental constituencies, and the public.

The Natural Resource Report Series is used to disseminate high-priority, current natural resource management information with managerial application. The series targets a general, diverse audience, and may contain NPS policy considerations or address sensitive issues of management applicability.

All manuscripts in the series receive the appropriate level of peer review to ensure that the information is scientifically credible, technically accurate, appropriately written for the intended audience, and designed and published in a professional manner.

This report received informal peer review by subject-matter experts who were not directly involved in the collection, analysis, or reporting of the data. Data in this report were collected and analyzed using methods based on established, peer-reviewed protocols and were analyzed and interpreted within the guidelines of the protocols.

Views, statements, findings, conclusions, recommendations, and data in this report do not necessarily reflect views and policies of the National Park Service, U.S. Department of the Interior. Mention of trade names or commercial products does not constitute endorsement or recommendation for use by the U.S. Government.

This report is available from the Heartland I&M Network website (http://www.nature.nps.gov/im/units/htln) on the internet and the Natural Resource Publications Management website (http://www.nature.nps.gov/publications/nrpm/).

Please cite this publication as:

Young, C. C, J. C. Bell, C. S. Gross, and A. D. Dunkle. 2012. Invasive exotic plant monitoring (Year 2) and treatment recommendations for Lincoln Boyhood National Memorial. Natural Resource Report NPS/HTLN/NRR—2012/569. National Park Service, Fort Collins, Colorado.

NPS 422/116829, September 2012

Contents

Figures

Figures (continued)

Tables

Executive Summary

We conducted a second year of invasive plant surveys at Lincoln Boyhood National Memorial. This allowed a comparison of invasive plant species found in 2006 to those found in 2011. To make this comparison, we walked along transects that spanned the entire park and searched for 104 plant species that we identified as potentially present and potentially problematic on the park. During the surveys, we found 42 of these species. We did not view the changes in plant frequency as indiciative of any great increases on the park. Issues related to observer bias prevented us from relying strongly on plant cover data as indicative of change. Given this caveat, our interpretation was that only three species may have increased in terms of plant cover. Distinctive guilds of invasive species were identified that included woody plants, grasses, and forbs.

 In some cases, cultural landscapes require invasive plant management treatments to maintain these historic sites. Based on our reading of the cultural landscape report, an evaluation of each plant's abundance and distribution in the park, and consideration of the biology of each species, we recommend specific treatments for 9 of 42 invasive plant species identified in this study, although all invasive plants detract from the forest as an important feature of the cultural landscape in the park. The decision to treat each species was not determined by a formula, but was assisted by characterizing the purpose of management for each species using a series of scenarios (Appendix A). In our opinion, these recommendations are in accordance with the treatments outlined the cultural landscape report, but require further evaluation through the National Environmental Policy Act and National Historical Preservation Act processes.

Acknowledgments

We thank Marla McEnaney, Lloyd Morrison, Ph.D., Mike DeBacker, and Mike Capps for helpful reviews.

Introduction

Forest Vegetation in Lincoln Boyhood National Memorial

The forest vegetation forms an important element of the cultural landscape of Lincoln Boyhood National Memorial (LIBO), along with several other contributing features: Nancy Hanks Lincoln's gravesite within the pioneer cemetery, the flagpole terrace, the allee, the plaza, the memorial building and court, the cabin site memorial, and the Trail of Twelve Stones (McEnaney 2001). Rather than simply serving as a natural area, the forest as intended by Frederick Law Olmsted, Jr. should represent the forest encountered by pioneers and "be considered equal in importance to the allee, cabin site memorial, or Trail of Twelve Stones" (McEnaney 2001). In particular, the forest frames the gravesite and purposefully contrasts with the open view along the allee and terrace. The use of native plants on the site, including in the surrounding forest, was an intentional landscape element designed to maintain the connection with the American frontier landscape found in Indiana. Given the extensive disturbance of the landscape features on the site, Olmsted also noted, when designing the site, that only the forests could be recreated "without sham or falsehood". Taking these considerations in to account, the forest is clearly part of the cultural landscape, which contributes significantly to the ranking of the park's integrity as medium to high (McEnaney 2001).

Oaks and hickories presumably dominated the forest canopy prior to settlement; Olmsted noted this when designing the memorial (McEnaney 2001). Notes from the General Land Office in 1805 showed that within a 3-mile radius of the site, white oak (*Quercus alba*), black oak (*Q. velutina*), and hickories (*Carya* spp.) accounted for over 60% of the trees recorded during the survey (Pavlovic and White 1989). After claiming 160 acres in 1816, Tom Lincoln worked to clear the site, preparing it for cultivation. As this part of Indiana developed as a patchwork of forests and farms, aerial photographs from 1937 showed that the park was largely cleared with the exception of a patch of forest in the vicinity of the gravesite (McEnaney 2001, Pavlovic and White 1989). The larger trees in this area were estimated at that time to be over 145 years old. Civilian Conservation Corps teams replanted much of the area in the park located east of County Road 300 and south of Lewis Street during the 1930's. Although records of the exact planting mix are unknown, the current composition indicates that plantings consisted largely of red maple (*Acer rubrum*), sugar maple (*Acer saccharum*), and tulip tree (*Liriodendron tulipifera*) rather than oaks or hickories. Outside of this area, succession has led to forests in which red maple, sassafras (*Sassafras alibidum*), sweetgum (*Liquidambar styraciflua*), and tulip tree dominate.

The Pavlovic and White (1989) report pointed to the need for invasive plant management exclusively within the larger context of forest restoration. For example, Japanese honeysuckle was recognized as ubiquitous and possibly responsible for decreasing herbaceous diversity. The absence of Japanese honeysuckle from the old growth hardwood forests was also noted as a condition that should be maintained. Sugar maple and tulip tree, while native to the U.S., were identified as potential introductions on the site and frequently suggested as targets for control to promote oak and hickory regeneration. The recommended approach, in this case, was to focus such control in small gaps cut into the existing canopy. Forsythia (*Forsythia suspensa*) and common periwinkle (*Vinca minor*) control was identified as a need in the vicinity of the cemetery to increase herbaceous plant cover and diversity. Despite these recommendations, Pavlovic and White described their studies as encountering "few exotic tree or shrub species" – among those identified included white pine (*Pinus strobus*), common privet (*Ligustrum vulgare*), and mock orange (*Philadelphus coronarius*). Finally, treatment of lawns of exotic cool season grasses such as fescue (*Festuca* spp.) was designed to accelerate succession towards forest.

In our judgment, the focus on restoration in the cultural landscape report and Pavlovic-White report is a highly strategic approach to management of the forest. Given that these restoration actions have not been implemented, however, the question regarding invasive species more broadly remains open. In the absence of a more comprehensive plan, we used a series of invasive plant management scenarios (see Appendix 1) to guide invasive plant treatment recommendations for the forest in Lincoln Boyhood National Memorial. These recommendations do not apply to the allee, plaza, memorial building and court, or cabin site memorial.

Methods

Watch lists

Invasive exotic plant species on three watch lists were sought during monitoring (Table 1). Plants designated as high priority invasive plant species (Young et al. 2007a) and known to occur in the same state as the park, but not on the park per NPSpecies (NPS 2012) constituted the "early detection watch list" (n=75). Designated invasive plants known to occur on the park per NPSpecies constituted the "park-established watch list" (n=25). Invasive exotic plants constituting the "park-based watch list" (n=5) included plants selected by park managers or network staff that were not designated as invasive in the protocol, but may not have been included due to incomplete information in NPSpecies (i.e., not documented) or inaccurate information in the USDA Plants database (i.e., state distribution information inaccurate) or simply due to differing opinions regarding Heartland Network's designation. These plant species were also non-native with the exception of black locust, which is native to the United States, but not to south-central Indiana.

Field methods

Invasive plant species were sought in search units that covered the park except for developed areas (Figure 1). Dan Tenaglia conducted field work from August 8-11, 2006 using a MobileMapper GPS Unit. Dr. Steven Brewer with Copperhead Consulting and Ms. Kyla Hershey with Lawhon and Associates, Inc. used a Garmin 60CSx and Trimble Instruments model GeoXT handheld GPS units to conduct the second survey during August 8-14, 2011. Surveys were conducted in search units, approximately 2 acres in size. Three equidistant transects through each search unit were surveyed; entire polygons were not fully searched. Observers surveyed invasive plants within a 3- to 12-m. Cover values were as follows: 0=0, 1=0.1-0.9 m^2, 2=1-9.9 m^2, 3=10-49.9 m^2, 4= 50-99.9 m^2, 5=100-499.9 m^2, 6= 500-999.9 m^2, 7= 1000-4,999.9 m^2. A total of 321 transects within 107 search units were searched.

Analytical methods

A park-wide cover range was estimated for each invasive plant species encountered. First, calculations of the observed reference frame fraction were made by multiplying transect length, the number of transects, and the belt width. The belt width was either 3 m (the minimum possible width) or 12 m (the maximum possible width). Transect length was calculated by summing the lengths of the 321 transects. The product was then divided by the reference frame area (Eq. 1).

Eq.1. Fraction of area searched = $\dfrac{\textit{transect length * number of transects * belt width}}{\textit{reference frame area}}$

The minimum fraction of area searched (belt width = 3 m) was 10%, and the maximum fraction of area searched (belt width = 12 m) was 40%.

To calculate the minimum of the estimated cover range for each species, the lower endpoints associated with the assigned cover class values for that species were summed and then divided by the reference frame fraction observed assuming the widest possible survey belt (i.e., maximum fraction observed) (Eq. 2).

Eq.2. Minimum cover estimate = $\dfrac{\Sigma \, low \, end \, of \, cover \, value \, range \, for \, species}{fraction \, of \, area \, searched \, assuming \, 12\text{-}m \, belt \, width}$

Maximum cover for each species was calculated similarly, summing the upper endpoints of the cover values in each occupied search unit and assuming that a 3-m belt was surveyed (i.e., minimum fraction of area observed) (Eq. 3).

Eq. 3. Maximum cover estimate = $\dfrac{\Sigma \, high \, end \, of \, cover \, value \, range \, for \, species}{fraction \, of \, area \, searched \, assuming \, 3\text{-}m \, belt \, width}$

The park-wide frequency of invasive exotic plants was then calculated as the percentage of occupied search units (Eq. 4).

Eq. 4. Frequency of an invasive plant species = $\dfrac{\Sigma \, search \, units \, occupied \, by \, species}{\Sigma \, search \, units \, sampled} \times 100$

Finally, maps were created for each target invasive plant species. The maps indicated which search unit was occupied and the estimated cover class value for that search unit. Note that entire search units were not fully searched.

Taken together, the minimum and maximum cover estimates provide an estimated range of cover that accounts for the uncertainty arising from the sampling method. Non-overlapping ranges represent the strongest evidence for differences in abundance.

Invasiveness ranks

In order to provide additional information on the ecological impact and feasibility of control, the ecological impact and general management difficulty sub-ranks that constituted the invasiveness rank (I-rank), as determined by NatureServe (Morse et al. 2004), were listed when available. The ecological impact characterizes the effect of the plant on ecosystem processes, community composition and structure, native plant and animal populations, and the conservation significance of threatened biodiversity. General management difficulty ranks are assigned based on the resources and time generally required to control a plant, the non-target effects of control on native populations, and the accessibility of invaded sites. Sub-ranks are given as high (H), medium (M), low (L), insignificant (I), unknown (U), or a combination of ranks.

Lincoln Boyhood National Memorial
Exotic Plant Search Units

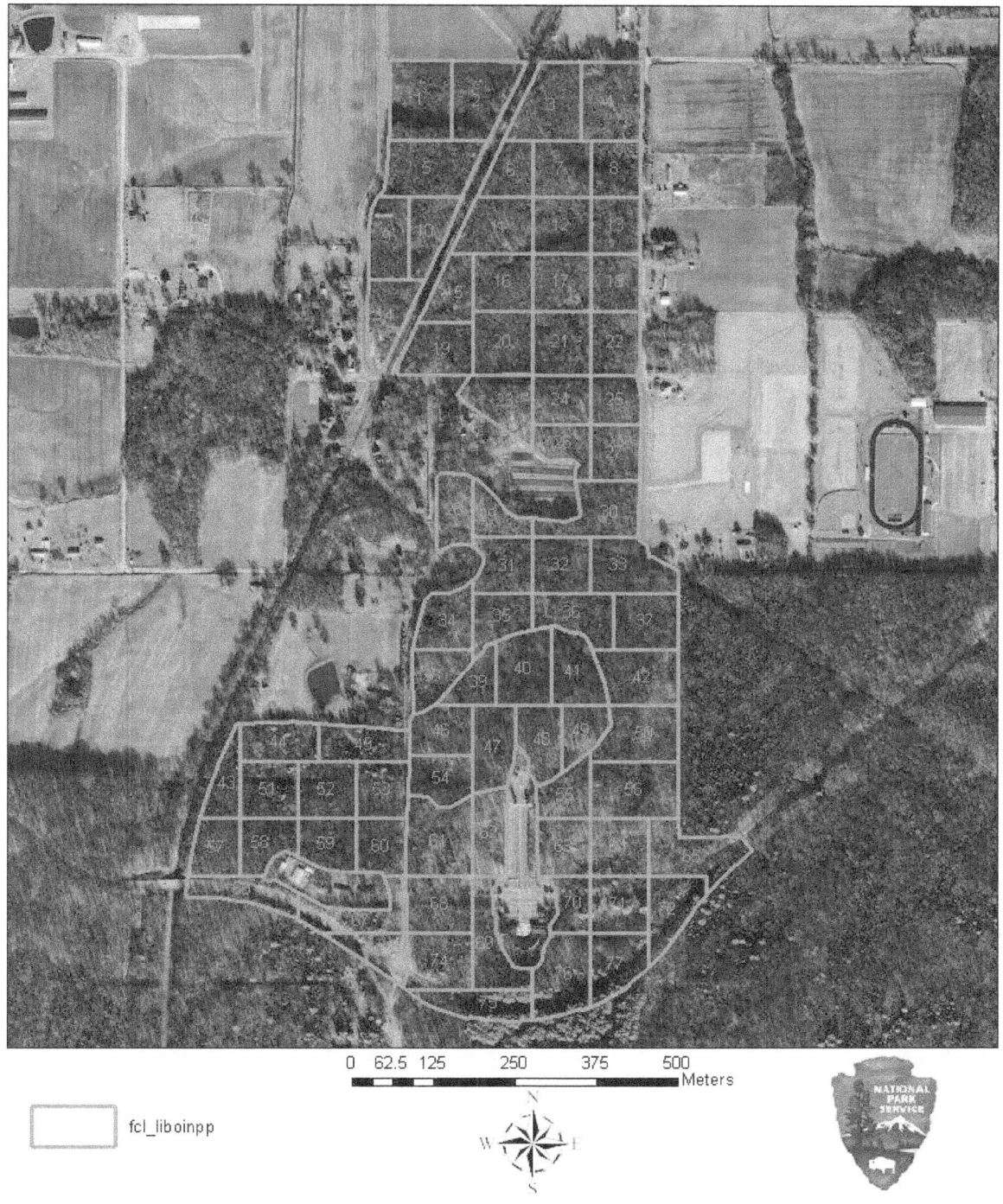

Figure 1. Invasive exotic plant search units at Lincoln Boyhood National Memorial. The search units indicate the search locations for invasive exotic plants in 2006 and 2011.

Results and Discussion

We identified a cumulative total of 42 out of 104 (40%) invasive plant species sought during both surveys (Table 2). Of these, 15 (20%) invasive plant species occurred on the early detection watch list of 74 species; 22 (88%) species were noted from the park-established watch list of 25 species; and all five park-based watch list species were found.

Invasive Plant Frequency

Invasive plant species were widespread in Lincoln Boyhood National Memorial. Of the 26 species found during both surveys, 7 species (27%) occupied at least 20% of search units in 2011, while 11 (42%) occupied less than 5% of search units. Overall, the frequency increased for 54% and decreased for 38% of these species from 2006 to 2011. Of the 16 species found during only a single survey, 15 (94%) occupied less than 5% of search units in 2011. Tall fescue, identified in 13% of search units, was likely overlooked during 2006 surveys as the species was not recorded during that survey. Based on these results, we did not discern any general increase in plant frequency. The limited distribution of several species suggests that control efforts may successfully eradicate or reduce these plants, although we recognize that only 10%-40% of the total area was searched.

Invasive Plant Abundance

Between 2006 and 2011, cover was noted as higher for the great majority of invasive plant species found in Lincoln Boyhood National Memorial (Table 2). The consistency in the direction and magnitude of these increases suggested strong observer differences between years rather than actual increases. In spite of this observer error, the abundance ranks remained somewhat ordered with seven of the ten most abundant species in 2006 also being among the ten most abundant in 2011. In 2011, maximum potential cover of 7 invasive exotic plants exceeded 10 acres; 22 of the 35 invasive species recorded in 2011 occupied at most less than 2 acres.

Given the strong observer differences, we largely ignored these differences and assumed that non-overlapping abundance estimates might still provide an indicator of change in abundance between time periods. Based on non-overlapping cover ranges, we identified three species as increasing from the 2006 survey: Japanese knotweed, Japanese barberry, and bluegrass. An additional 9 species that were not found in at all in 2006 may also represent increases in abundance. We interpreted the rest of the overlapping ranges as reflecting general similarity in abundance between 2006 and 2011.

Biological Considerations Affecting Invasive Plant Management Decisions

In contrast to the few invasive shrub and tree species found on the park in the late 1980's (Pavlovic and White 1989), we found numerous invasive woody plant species. Several of these species occupied at least 0.2 acres including Autumn olive (*Elaeagnus umbellata*), black locust (*Robinia pseudoacacia*), European privet (*Ligustrum vulgare*), multiflora rose (*Rosa multiflora*), and weeping forsythia (*Forsythia suspensa*). Other woody species included amur honeysuckle (*Lonicera maackii*), border privet (*Ligustrum obtusifolium*), burning bush (*Euonymus alata*), Callery pear (*Pyrus calleryana*), Chinese privet (*Ligustrum sinense*), Japanese barberry (*Berberis thunbergii*), Morrow's honeysuckle (*Lonicera morrowii*), silktree (aka mimosa, *Albizia julibrissin*), spiraea (*Spiraea* spp.), tree-of-heaven (*Ailanthus altissima*), and white mulberry (*Morus alba*). Only autumn olive was characterized as having an unambiguously high ecological impact rank. With the exception of European privet and spiraea, management difficulty for all other woody species is medium or less. This ranking likely reflects the fact that cut stump and basal bark treatment methods allow these species to be controlled with little damage to surrounding plants.

Invasive grasses constituted a second group of invasive plants present on the park. These were predominantly cool season (i.e., C_3) grasses. For example, tall fescue (*Schedonorus phoenix*) is the most prevalent species occupying at least 0.8 acres. Other lawn-forming cool season grasses included bald brome (*Bromus racemosus*), Kentucky bluegrass (*Poa pratensis*), perennial ryegrass (*Lolium perenne*), and orchardgrass (*Dactylis glomerata*). The impact of these species is medium, and management difficulty (with the possible exception of tall fescue) is medium or less. Reed canarygrass (*Phalaris arundinacea*), a cool season grass occupying at least 0.06 acres, was first detected in 2011 and may be difficult to control. This plant inhabits wetlands and areas with wet to moist soil. Two invasive warm season (i.e., C_4) grasses with contrasting habitat requirements also occur in Lincoln Boyhood National Memorial. Johnsongrass (*Sorghum halespense*) occupies no more than 0.3 acres in open sites with high light, while Japanese stiltgrass (*Microstegium vimineum*), which colonizes and spreads beneath intact forest canopies, occupies at least 0.3 acres. Johnsongrass was detected in 2006, but not in 2011. Japanese stiltgrass was estimated to occupy at least 0.3 acres in 2011. Both species may be difficult to control.

Vines and vining herbaceous plants comprised a third widespread guild of invasive plants. These species may reflect the legacy of Lincoln City and surrounding home sites prior to early establishment of the memorial site. The two most abundant and fourth most abundant invasive plant species in the park – Japanese honeysuckle (*Lonicera japonica*), common periwinkle (*Vinca minor*), and winter creeper (*Euonymus fortunei*), respectively – belong to this class of plants. Other invasive vines included Chinese wisteria (*Wisteria sinensis*), Chinese yam (*Dioscorea villosa*), English ivy (*Hedera helix*), and oriental bittersweet (*Celastrus orbiculatus*). The ecological impact and management difficulty of all vines, except for Japanese honeysuckle, does not exceed medium. Difficulty of Japanese honeysuckle, a ubiquitous species at LIBO, may be high, most likely due to its tendency to intertwine with surrounding plants. The evergreen or semi-evergreen nature of many invasive vine species, including Japanese honeysuckle, presents opportunities to apply chemical controls during early spring and late fall after the majority of the other plants have not yet begun to grow or have senesced, respectively.

Relatively few herbaceous species pose significant management problems from a biological perspective. For example, only Japanese knotweed is abundant, covering at least 0.7 acres, and is the only herbaceous plant with potentially high management difficulty. All other herbs cover less than a maximum of 0.5 acres. Actual cover is likely much lower. All other species except crown vetch (*Securigera varia*) were ranked as having ecological impacts and management difficulty of medium or less with the vast majority of species ranked as possibly low or even insignificant. Fortunately, the high ecological impact of crown vetch is matched with low management difficulty.

Recommended Landscape Maintenance Treatments Related to Invasive Plants
Our reading of the cultural landscape report suggests that all non-native plant species should be removed from the forest at Lincoln Boyhood National Memorial to the extent practicable. This

contention reflects the aim of the forest by design (McEnaney 2001) to support plant species typical of the period of the Lincoln homestead. These actions designed to protect the cultural landscape may best be described as "weeding" projects (Young et al. 2012, Appendix 1) that would be required to maintain horticultural plantings or gardens. The relatively small size of the park makes this goal more realistic than if applied to a larger area such as the adjacent Lincoln State Park.

Despite the clear justification for such work, the large number of invasive plant species requires that we prioritize control actions by area and by species (Table 2). First, we propose controlling all woody species and most vines in the vicinity of Nancy Hank's gravesite because of its importance within the cultural landscape. The difficulty in controlling Japanese honeysuckle, which may require hand-pulling, leads us to propose that this species be controlled only within the "old-growth" upland oak-hickory forest. Secondly, throughout the park, we propose the control of invasive plant species known to spread within intact forests – garlic mustard and Japanese stiltgrass; those ranked as having high ecological impact while their distribution or abundance are still relatively low – amur honeysuckle, black locust, crown vetch, Japanese barberry, Japanese knotweed, and reed canarygrass; and those with high management difficulty, but highly treatable growth forms – European privet, Johnsongrass, and spiraea. Finally, we believe that delaying immediate treatment of the other species will not lead to damage of the cultural landscape or be appreciably more difficult and expensive in the near future.

Literature Cited

McEnaney, M. 2001. A noble avenue: Lincoln Boyhood National Memorial cultural landscape report. National Park Service, Midwest Regional Office unpublished report. Omaha, Nebraska.

Morse, L. E., J. M. Randall, N. Benton, R. D. Hiebert, and S. Lu. 2004. An Invasive Species Assessment Protocol: Evaluating Non-Native Plants for Their Impact on Biodiversity. Version 1. Document. Online. <http://www.natureserve.org/getData/plantData.jsp#InvasivesProtocol>. Accessed 1 December 2006.

NPSpecies - The National Park Service Biodiversity Database. IRMA version. https://irma.nps.gov/Species.mvc/Welcome (accessed 16 February 2012).

Pavlovic, N.B. and M. White. 1989. Forest restoration of Lincoln Boyhood National Memorial: Presettlement, existing vegetation and restoration management recommendations. Research/Resources Management Report MWR-15. National Park Service, Omaha, Nebraska.

Young, C.C., J.L. Haack, L.W. Morrison, and M.D. DeBacker. 2007. Invasive exotic plant monitoring protocol for the Heartland Inventory and Monitoring Program. Natural Resource Report NPS/HTLN/NRR-2007/018. National Park Service, Fort Collins, Colorado.

Young, C. C., J. C. Bell, C. S. Gross, and A. D. Dunkle. 2012. Invasive exotic plant monitoring (year 2) and treatment recommendation for Arkansas Post National Memorial. Natural Resource Technical Report NPS/HTLN/NRTR—2012/609. National Park Service, Fort Collins, Colorado

Table 1. Invasive plant watch lists.

Early Detection Watch List	
Scientific name	**Common name**
Acer platanoides	Norway maple
Alliaria petiolata	Garlic mustard
Alnus glutinosa	European alder
Arctium minus	Lesser burdock
Bromus inermis	Smooth brome
Bromus sterilis	Poverty brome
Bromus tectorum	Cheatgrass
Butomus umbellatus	Flowering rush
Carduus nutans	Nodding plumeless thistle
Celastrus orbiculatus	Oriental bittersweet
Centaurea solstitialis	Yellow star-thistle
Centaurea stoebe ssp. Micranthos	Spotted knapweed
Cirsium arvense	Canada thistle
Cirsium vulgare	Bull thistle
Cynanchum louiseae	Louise's swallow-wort
Cynanchum rossicum	European swallow-wort
Dipsacus fullonum	Fuller's teasel
Dipsacus laciniatus	Cutleaf teasel
Egeria densa	Brazilian waterweed
Elaeagnus umbellata	Autumn olive
Elymus repens	Quackgrass
Euonymus alata	Burningbush
Euphorbia cyparissias	Cypress spurge
Euphorbia esula	Leafy Spurge
Frangula alnus	Glossy buckthorn
Hesperis matronalis	Dames rocket
Holcus lanatus	Common velvetgrass
Humulus japonicus	Japanese hop
Hypericum perforatum	Common St. Johnswort
Iris pseudacorus	Paleyellow iris
Leonurus cardiaca	Common motherwort
Lepidium latifolium	Broadleaved pepperweed
Lespedeza bicolor	Shrub lesepedza
Linaria vulgaris	Butter and eggs
Lolium arundinaceum	Tall fescue
Lolium pratense	Meadow fescue
Lonicera maackii	Amur honeysuckle
Lonicera tatarica	Tatarian honeysuckle
Lonicera X bella	
Lotus corniculatus	Bird's-foot trefoil
Lysimachia nummularia	Creeping jenny
Lythrum salicaria	Purple loosestrife
Microstegium vimineum	Nepalese browntop
Miscanthus sinensis	Chinese silvergrass
Myosotis scorpioides	True forget-me-not
Myriophyllum spicatum	Eurasian watermilfoil
Najas minor	Brittle waternymph
Onopordum acanthium	Scotch cottonthistle
Ornithogalum umbellatum	Sleepydick
Pastinaca sativa	Wild parsnip
Paulownia tomentosa	Princesstree
Phalaris arundinacea	Reed canarygrass
Phragmites australis	Common reed
Populus alba	White poplar
Potamogeton crispus	Curly pondweed
Potentilla recta	Sulphur sinquefoil

Early Detection Watch List (continued)	
Prunus mahaleb	Mahaleb's cherry
Pueraria montana var. lobata	Kudzu
Pyrus calleryana	Callery pear
Rhamnus cathartica	Common buckthron
Rorippa nasturtium-aquaticum	Watercress
Rumex crispus	Curly dock
Saponaria officinalis	Bouncingbet
Sonchus arvensis	Field sowthistle
Securigera varia	Crownvetch
Sorghum halepense	Johnsongrass
Spiraea japonica	Japanese meadowsweet
Tanacetum vulgare	Common tansy
Torilis arvensis	Spreading hedgeparsley
Torilis japonica	Ercet hedgeparsley
Typha angustifolia	Narrowleaf cattail
Typha X glauca	
Ulmus pumila	Siberian elm
Viburnum opulus	European cranberrybush
Park-Established Watch List	
Ailanthus altissima	Tree of heaven
Albizia julibrissin	Silktree
Berberis thunbergii	Japanese barberry
Bromus racemosus	Bald brome
Daucus carota	Queen Anne's lace
Dioscorea oppositifolia	Chinese yam
Euonymus fortune	Winter creeper
Glechoma hederacea	Ground ivy
Hedera helix	English ivy
Hemerocallis fulva	Orange daylily
Lespedeza cuneata	Sericea lespedeza
Ligustrum obtusifolium	Border privet
Ligustrum vulgare	European privet
Lonicera japonica	Japanese honeysuckle
Lonicera morrowii	Morrow's honeysuckle
Melilotus officinalis	Sweetclover
Morus alba	White mulberry
Poa compressa	Canada bluegrass
Poa pratensis	Kentucky bluegrass
Polygonum cuspidatum	Japanese knotweed
Robinia pseudoacacia	Black locust
Rosa multiflora	Multiflora rose
Rumex acetosella	Common sheep sorrel
Verbascum thapsus	Common mullien
Vinca minor	Common periwinkle
Park-Based Watch List	
Dactylis glomerata	Bermudagrass
Forsythia suspensa	Weeping forsythia
Lolium perenne	Perennial ryegrass
Ligustrum sinense	Chinese privet
Wisteria sinensis	Chinese wisteria

Table 2. Overview of invasive exotic plants found in Lincoln Boyhood National Monument. Ecological impact and general management difficulty based on NatureServe I-Rank subranks, Morse et al. 2004. Subranks are given as high (H), medium (M), low (L), insignificant (I), unknown (U), a range of ranks (indicated by /), or not available (--).

Scientific Name	Common Name	Watch list	2006 Park-wide cover (acres)	2011 Park-wide cover (acres)	2006 Frequency (%)	2011 Frequency (%) (Frequency difference 2006-2011)	Ecological impact	Management difficulty
Lonicera japonica	Japanese honeysuckle	Park Established	1.6-19.5	8.4-146.0	68.2	72.0(3.8)	M	HM
Vinca minor	Common periwinkle	Park Established	0.7-10.8	4.4-72.0	17.8	20.6(2.8)	I	U
Rosa multiflora	Multiflora rose	Park Established	0.3-5.0	2.1-33.0	52.3	63.6(11.3)	L	L
Euonymus fortunei	Winter creeper	Park Established	0.06-0.9	0.9-17.8	23.4	28.0(4.6)	M	LI
Ligustrum vulgare	European privet	Park Established	0.3-5.4	1.0-16.5	49.5	56.1(6.6)	HL	HM
Schedonorus phoenix	Tall fescue	Park Established	--	0.8-16.4	0	13.1(13.1)	M	HM
Polygonum cuspidatum	Japanese knotweed	Park Established	0.008-0.2	0.7-12.8	4.7	3.7(-1)	HM	M
Microstegium vimineum	Nepalese browntop	Early Detection	0.06-0.9	0.3-5.2	18.7	20.6(1.9)	M	HM
Dioscorea oppositifolia	Chinese yam	Park Established	0.03-0.3	0.2-4.0	6.5	7.5(1)	ML	MI
Elaeagnus umbellata	Autumn olive	Early Detection	0.03-0.7	0.2-3.4	20.6	19.6(-1)	H	L
Robinia pseudoacacia	Black locust	Park Established	0.2-1.7	0.2-3.3	22.4	22.4(0)	HM	M
Forsythia suspensa	Weeping forsythia	Park Based	0.03-0.6	0.2-3.1	11.2	5.6(-5.6)	--	--
Hedera helix	English ivy	Park Established	0.02-0.3	0.2-2.8	4.7	3.7(-1)	M	ML
Albizia julibrissin	Silktree	Park Established	0.03-0.3	0.07-1.4	4.7	4.7(0)	ML	ML
Wisteria sinensis	Chinese wisteria	Park Based	0.007-0.2	0.07-1.4	2.8	3.7(0.9)	ML	L
Phalaris arundinacea	Reed canarygrass	Early Detection	--	0.06-1.2	0	0.9(0.9)	H	HM
Ailanthus altissima	Tree of heaven	Park Established	0.02-0.5	0.07-0.8	12.1	7.5(-4.6)	ML	ML
Lonicera maackii	Amur honeysuckle	Early Detection	0.001-0.05	0.04-0.8	2.8	6.5(3.7)	HM	M
Euonymus alata	Burningbush	Early Detection	0.04-0.4	0.03-0.7	7.5	11.2(3.7)	LI	L
Berberis thunbergii	Japanese barberry	Park Established	0.0001-0.02	0.03-0.6	6.5	7.5(1)	HM	I
Lysimachia nummularia	Creeping jenny	Early Detection	0.004-0.1	0.03-0.5	6.5	4.7(-1.8)	L	L
Morus alba	White mulberry	Park Established	--	0.04-0.4	0	1.9(1.9)	ML	ML
Spiraea (japonica)	Spiraea	Early Detection	0.09-0.8	0.04-0.4	3.7	1.9(-1.8)	ML	HM
Celastrus orbiculatus	Oriental bittersweet	Early Detection	0.01-0.4	0.01-0.3	26.2	6.5(-19.7)	ML	M

Table 2. (continued)

Scientific Name	Common Name	Watch list	2006 Park-wide cover (acres)	2011 Park-wide cover (acres)	2006 Frequency (%)	2011 Frequency (%) (Frequency difference 2006-2011)	Ecological impact	Management difficulty
Hemerocalis fulva	Orange daylily	Park Established	--	0.01-0.3	0	4.7(4.7)	MI	L
Alliaria petiolata	Garlic mustard	Early Detection	--	0.007-0.2	0	2.8(2.8)	ML	M
Poa (pratensis)	Kentucky bluegrass	Park Established	0.0001-0.004	0.007-0.2	1.9	2.8(0.9)	ML	HL
Bromus racemosus	Bald brome	Park Established	--	0.002-0.1	0	3.7(3.7)	MI	U
Pyrus calleryana	Callery pear	Early Detection	--	0.006-0.1	0	0.9(0.9)	LI	ML
Ligustrum obtusifolium	Border privet	Park Established	0.001-0.03	0.002-0.07	0.9	2.8(1.9)	LI	L
Cirsium vulgare	Bull thistle	Early Detection	0.0001-0.02	0.002-0.07	6.5	2.8(-3.7)	ML	ML
Lespedeza cuneata	Sericea lesedeza	Park Established	0.02-0.3	0.002-0.07	10.3	2.8(-7.5)	ML	ML
Daucus carota	Queen Anne's lace	Park Established	0.001-0.03	0.001-0.05	0.9	1.9(1)	I	I
Arctium minus	Lesser burdock	Early Detection	--	0.001-0.03	0	0.9(0.9)	LI	MI
Lolium perenne	Perennial ryegrass	Park Based	--	0.001-0.03	0	0.9(0.9)	M	MI
Sorghum halepense	Johnsongrass	Early Detection	0.03-0.3	--	0.9	0(-0.9)	ML	HM
Securigera varia	Crownvetch	Early Detection	0.001-0.05	--	1.9	0(-1.9)	H	L
Dactylis glomerata	Orchardgrass	Park Based	0.001-0.05	--	1.9	0(-1.9)	LI	ML
Lonicera morrowii	Morrow's honeysuckle	Park Established	0.001-0.03	--	2.8	0(-2.8)	ML	M
Lotus corniculatus	Bird's foot trefoil	Early Detection	0.001-0.03	--	0.9	0(-0.9)	ML	ML
Ligustrum sinense	Chinese privet	Park Based	0.0001-0.004	--	1.9	0(-1.9)	M	L
Verbascum thapsus	Common mullein	Park Established	0.0001-0.002	--	0.9	0(-0.9)	ML	L

Table 3. Treatment recommendations for invasive exotic plants in Lincoln Boyhood National Memorial.

Common Name	Treatment Recommendation
Amur honeysuckle	Cut stump treatment using triclopyr or imazapyr.
Black locust	Cut stump treatment using triclopyr or imazapyr.
Crown vetch	Spot treat isolated clumps with aminopyralid.
European privet	Cut stump treatment using triclopyr or imazapyr.
Garlic mustard	Treat in spring or fall with glyphosate + non-ionic surfactant.
Japanese barberry	Foliar treatment using triclopyr + a non-ionic surfactant or basal oil.
Japanese honeysuckle	Hand pull or foliar spray with triclopyr + non-ionic surfactant or basal oil.
Japanese knotweed	Spot treat with aquatic-safe glyphosate.
Japanese stiltgrass	Spot treat with aquatic-safe glyphosate or sethoxydin depending on proximity to water.
Johnsongrass	Spot treat with glyphosate, sethoxydin, or imazapyr depending on proximity to water.
Reed canarygrass	Spot treat with aquatic-safe glyphosate.
Spiraea	Cut stump treatment using triclopyr or imazapyr.

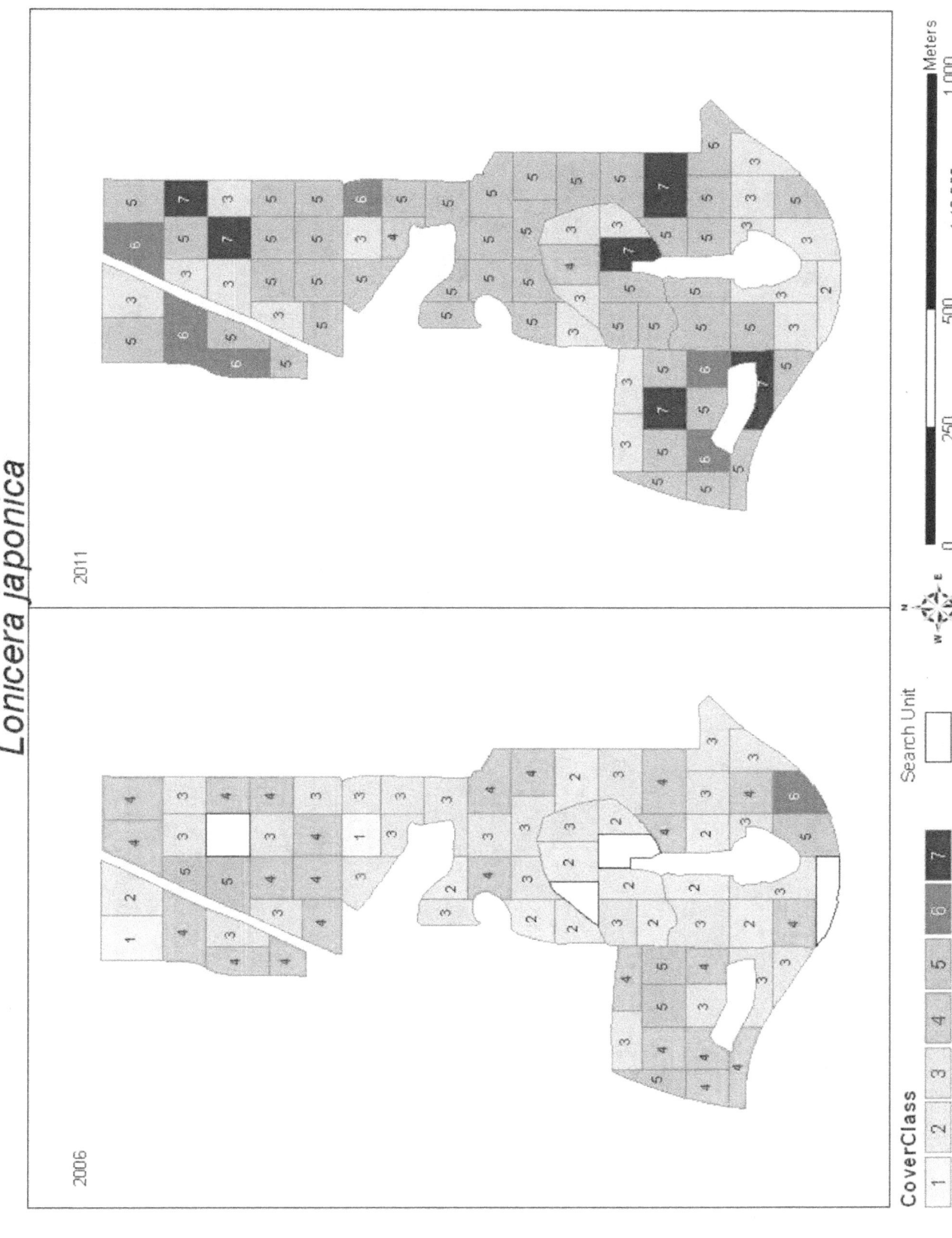

Lonicera japonica

2011

2006

Figure 2. Abundance and distribution of *Lonicera japonica* (Japanese honeysuckle) at Lincoln Boyhood National Memorial, 2006 and 2011. Cover classes are as follows: 1=0.1-0.9 m^2, 2=1-9.9 m^2, 3=10-49.9 m^2, 4= 50-99.9 m^2, 5=100-499.9 m^2, 6= 500-999.9 m^2, 7= 1,000-4,999 m^2.

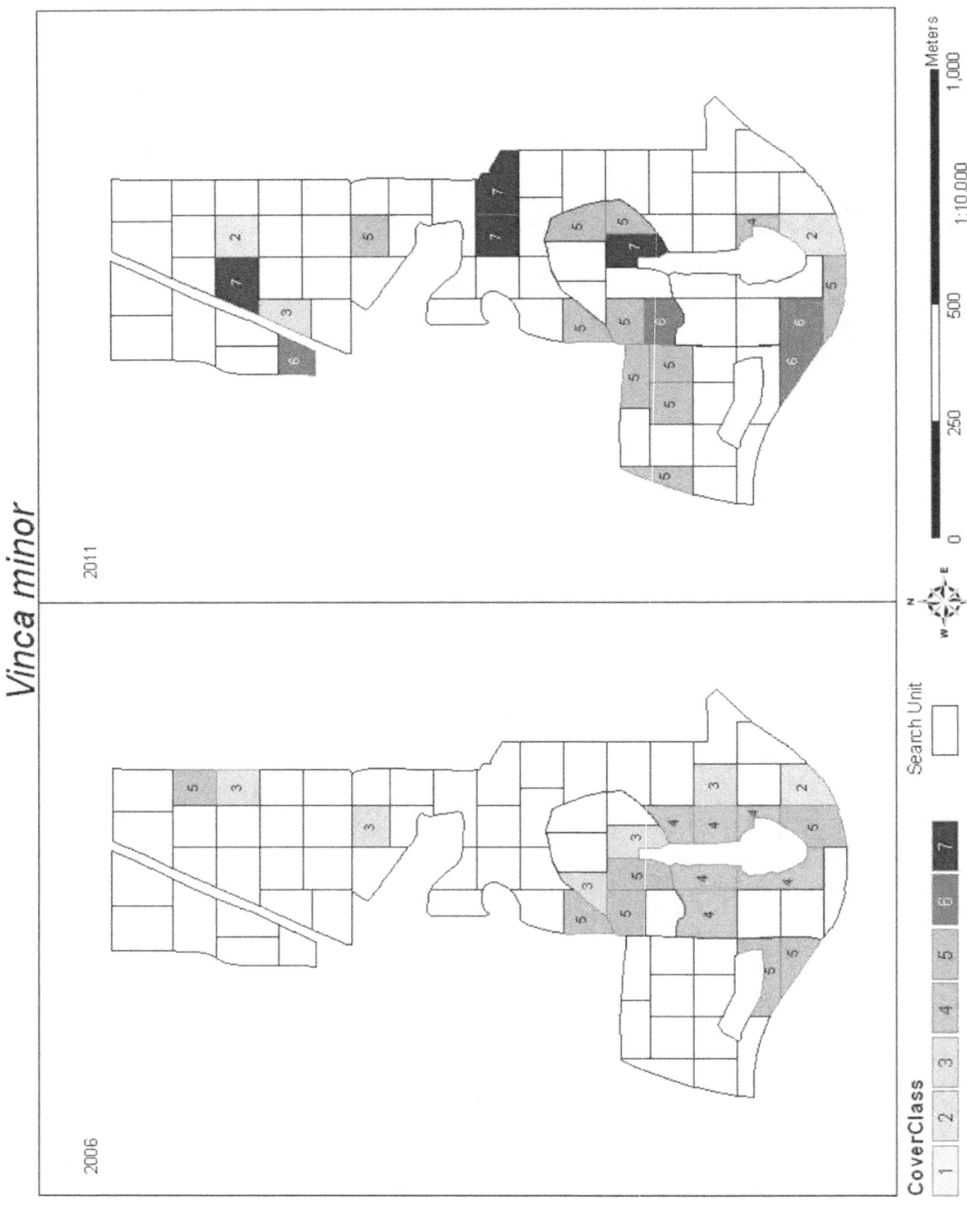

Figure 3. Abundance and distribution of *Vinca minor* (common periwinkle) at Lincoln Boyhood National Memorial, 2006 and 2011. Cover classes are as follows: 1=0.1-0.9 m^2, 2=1-9.9 m^2, 3=10-49.9 m^2, 4= 50-99.9 m^2, 5=100-499.9 m^2, 6= 500-999.9 m^2, 7= 1,000-4,999 m^2.

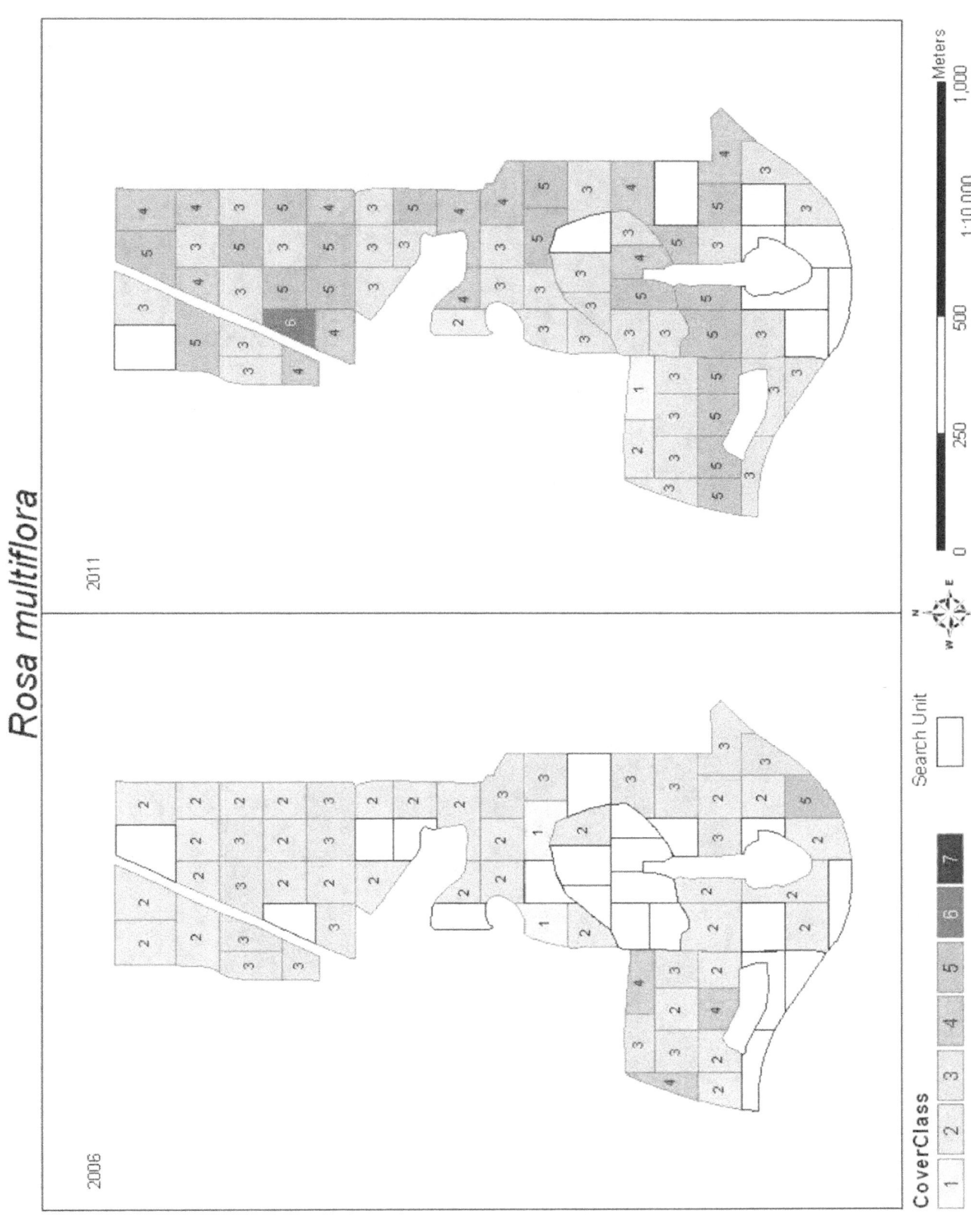

Figure 4. Abundance and distribution of *Rosa multiflora* (multiflora rose) at Lincoln Boyhood National Memorial, 2006 and 2011. Cover classes are as follows: 1=0.1-0.9 m^2, 2=1-9.9 m^2, 3=10-49.9 m^2, 4= 50-99.9 m^2, 5=100-499.9 m^2, 6= 500-999.9 m^2, 7= 1,000-4,999 m^2.

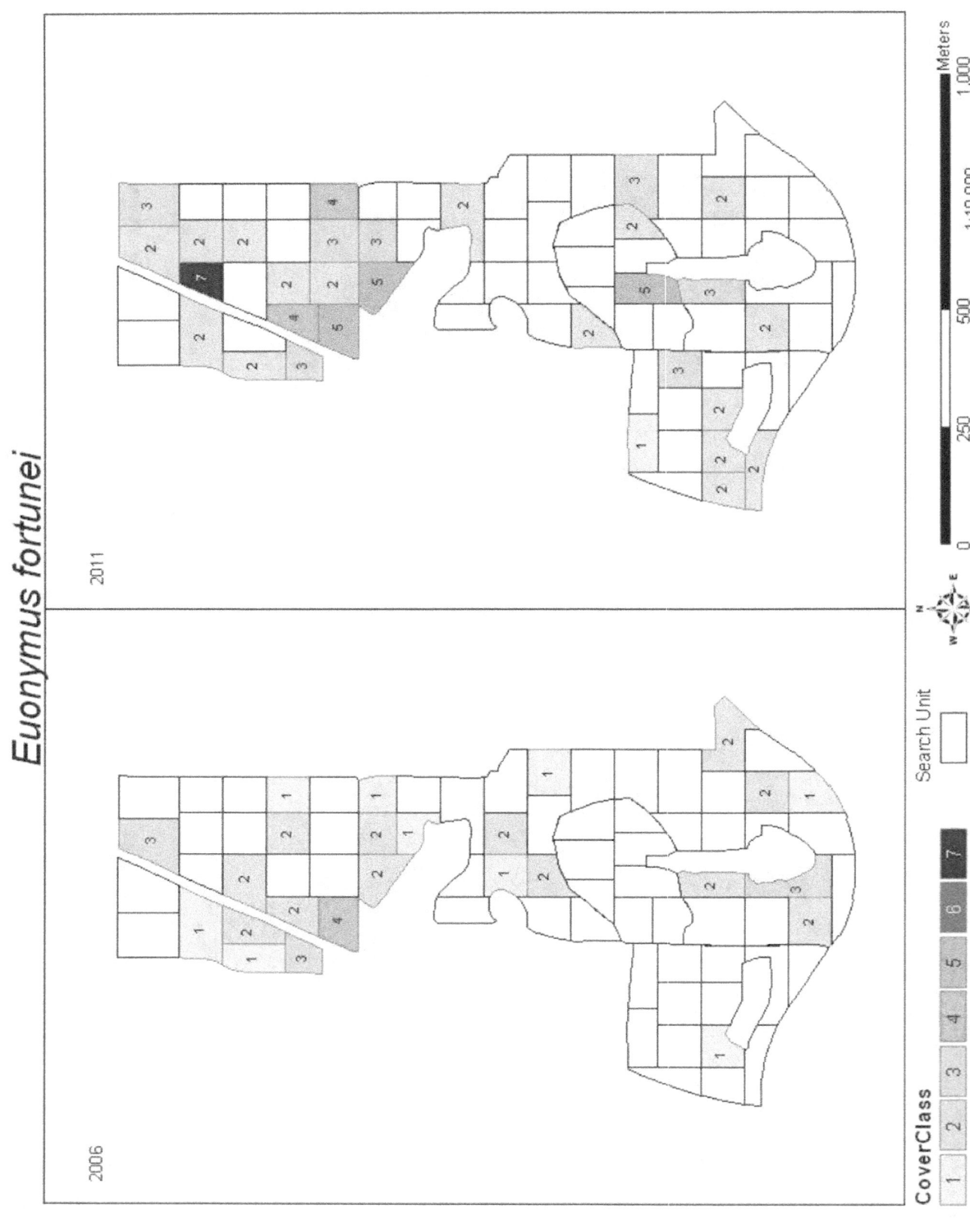

Figure 5. Abundance and distribution of *Euonymus fortunei* (wintercreeper) at Lincoln Boyhood National Memorial, 2006 and 2011. Cover classes are as follows: 1=0.1-0.9 m^2, 2=1-9.9 m^2, 3=10-49.9 m^2, 4= 50-99.9 m^2, 5=100-499.9 m^2, 6= 500-999.9 m^2, 7= 1,000-4,999 m^2.

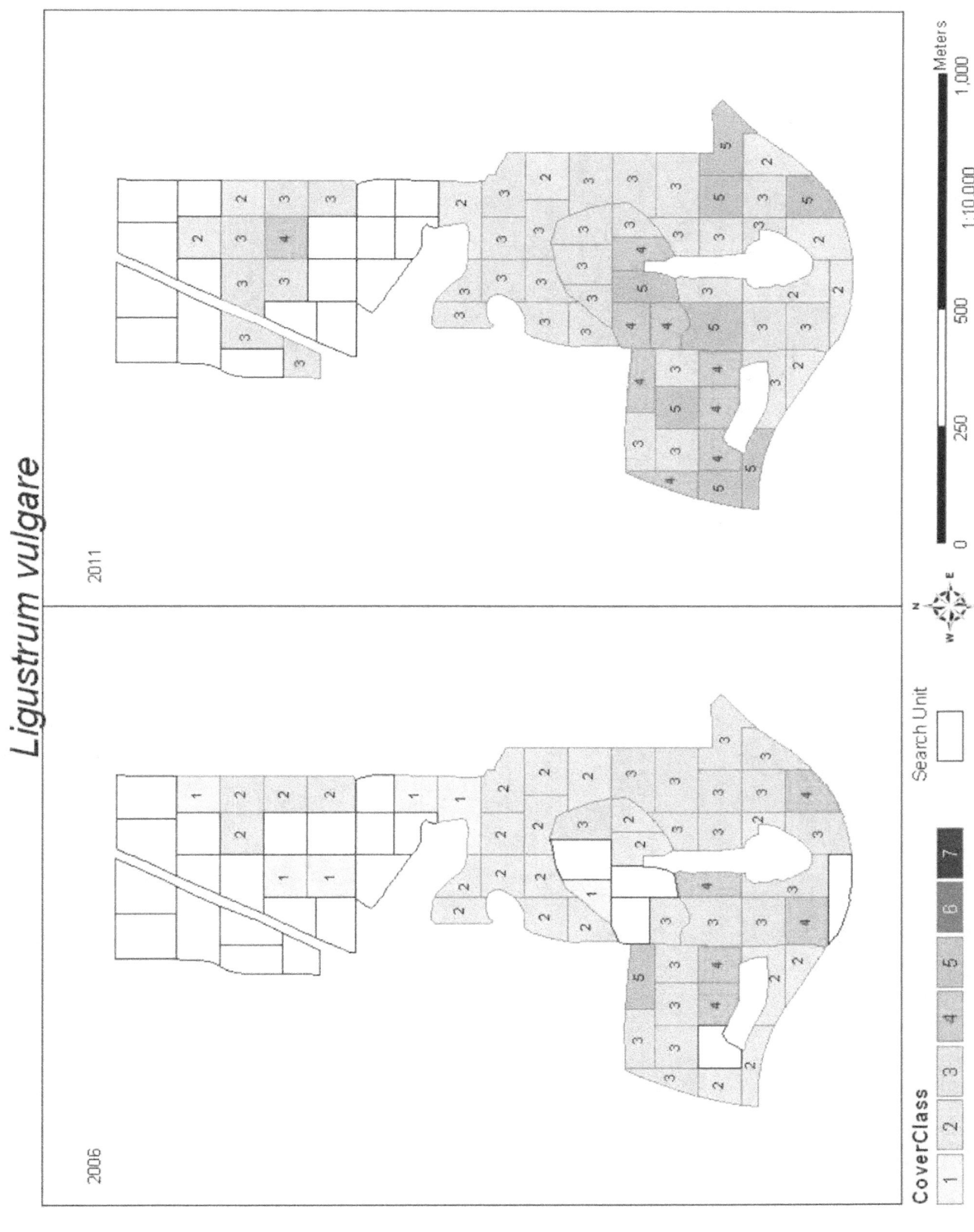

Figure 6. Abundance and distribution of *Ligustrum vulgare* (European privet) at Lincoln Boyhood National Memorial, 2006 and 2011. Cover classes are as follows: $1=0.1\text{-}0.9\ m^2$, $2=1\text{-}9.9\ m^2$, $3=10\text{-}49.9\ m^2$, $4=50\text{-}99.9\ m^2$, $5=100\text{-}499.9\ m^2$, $6=500\text{-}999.9\ m^2$, $7=1,000\text{-}4,999\ m^2$.

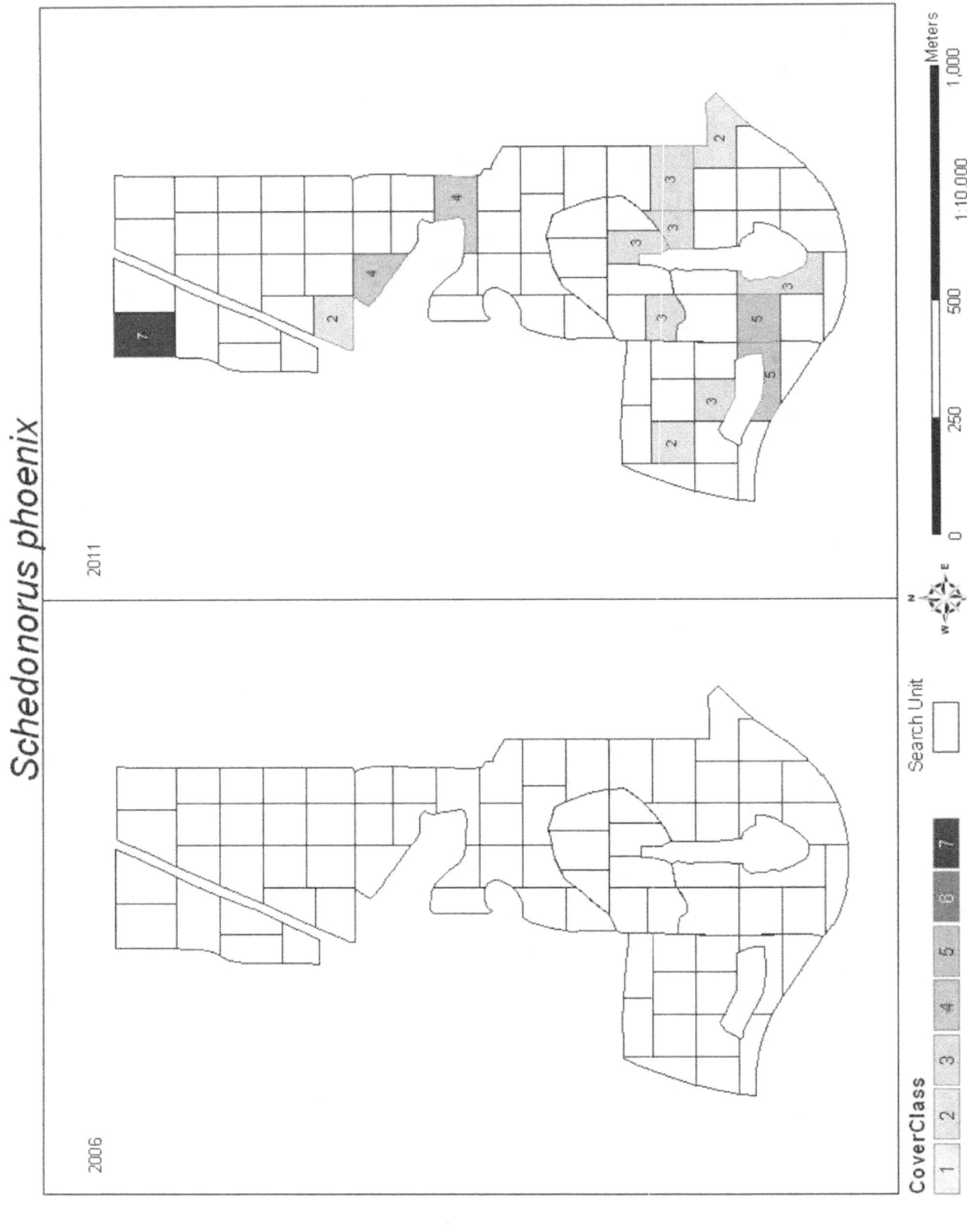

Figure 7. Abundance and distribution of *Schedonorus phoenix* (tall fescue) at Lincoln Boyhood National Memorial, 2006 and 2011. Cover classes are as follows: 1=0.1-0.9 m², 2=1-9.9 m², 3=10-49.9 m², 4= 50-99.9 m², 5=100-499.9 m², 6= 500-999.9 m², 7= 1,000-4,999 m².

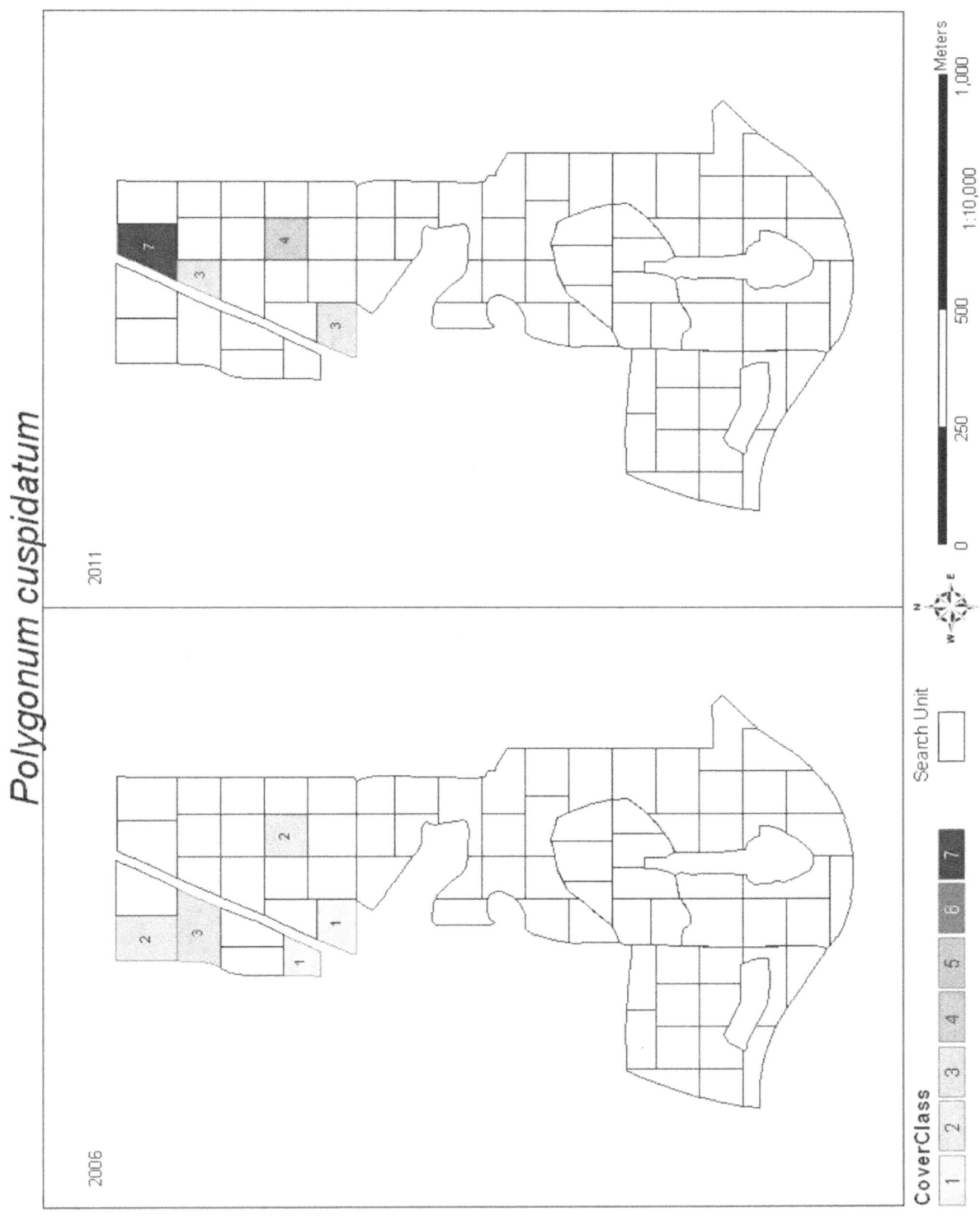

Polygonum cuspidatum

Figure 8. Abundance and distribution of *Polygonum cuspidatum* (Japanese knotweed) at Lincoln Boyhood National Memorial, 2006 and 2011. Cover classes are as follows: 1=0.1-0.9 m², 2=1-9.9 m², 3=10-49.9 m², 4= 50-99.9 m², 5=100-499.9 m², 6= 500-999.9 m², 7= 1,000-4,999 m².

21

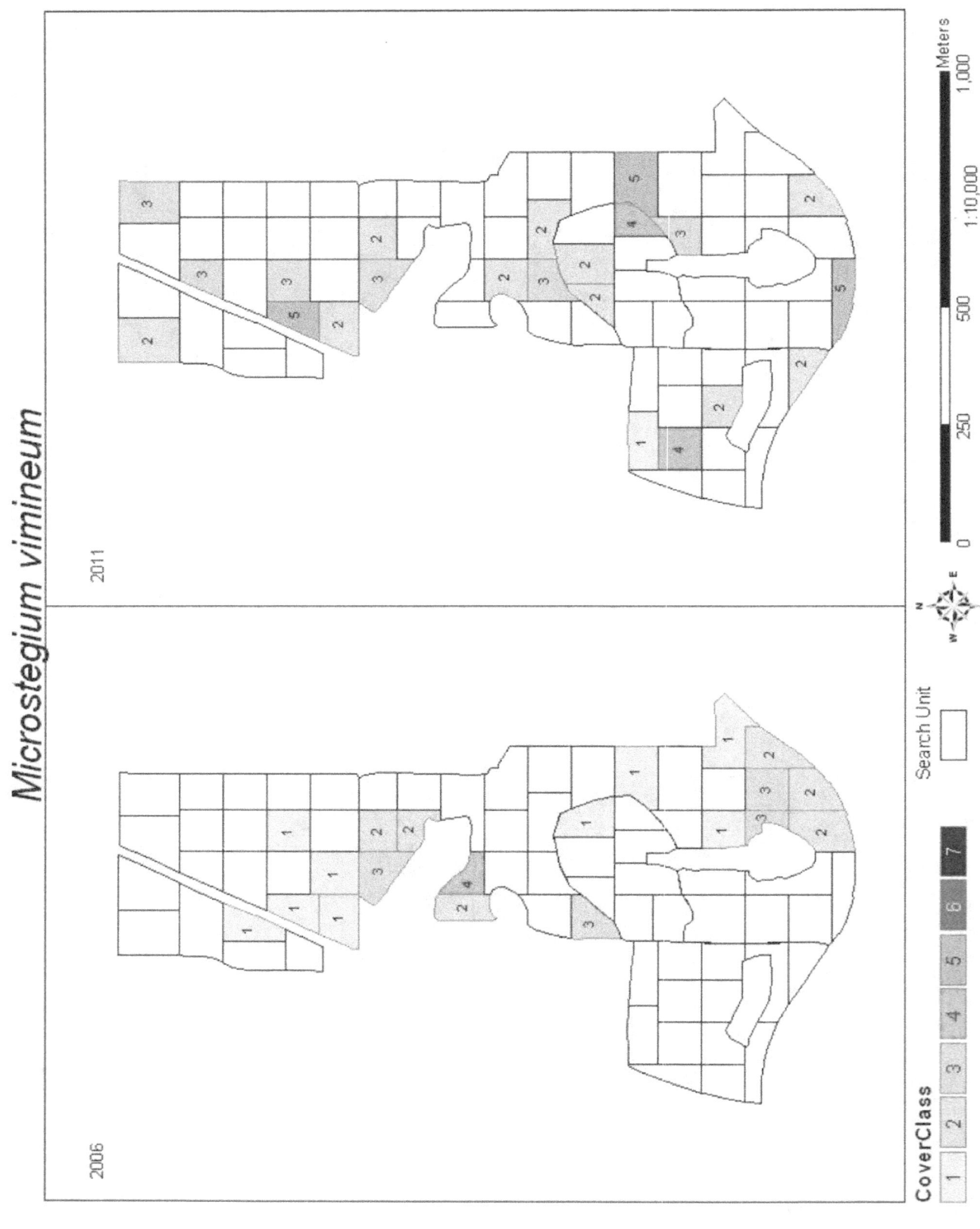

Figure 9. Abundance and distribution of *Microstegium vimineum* (Nepalese browntop) at Lincoln Boyhood National Memorial, 2006 and 2011. Cover classes are as follows: 1=0.1-0.9 m², 2=1-9.9 m², 3=10-49.9 m², 4= 50-99.9 m², 5=100-499.9 m², 6= 500-999.9 m², 7= 1,000-4,999 m².

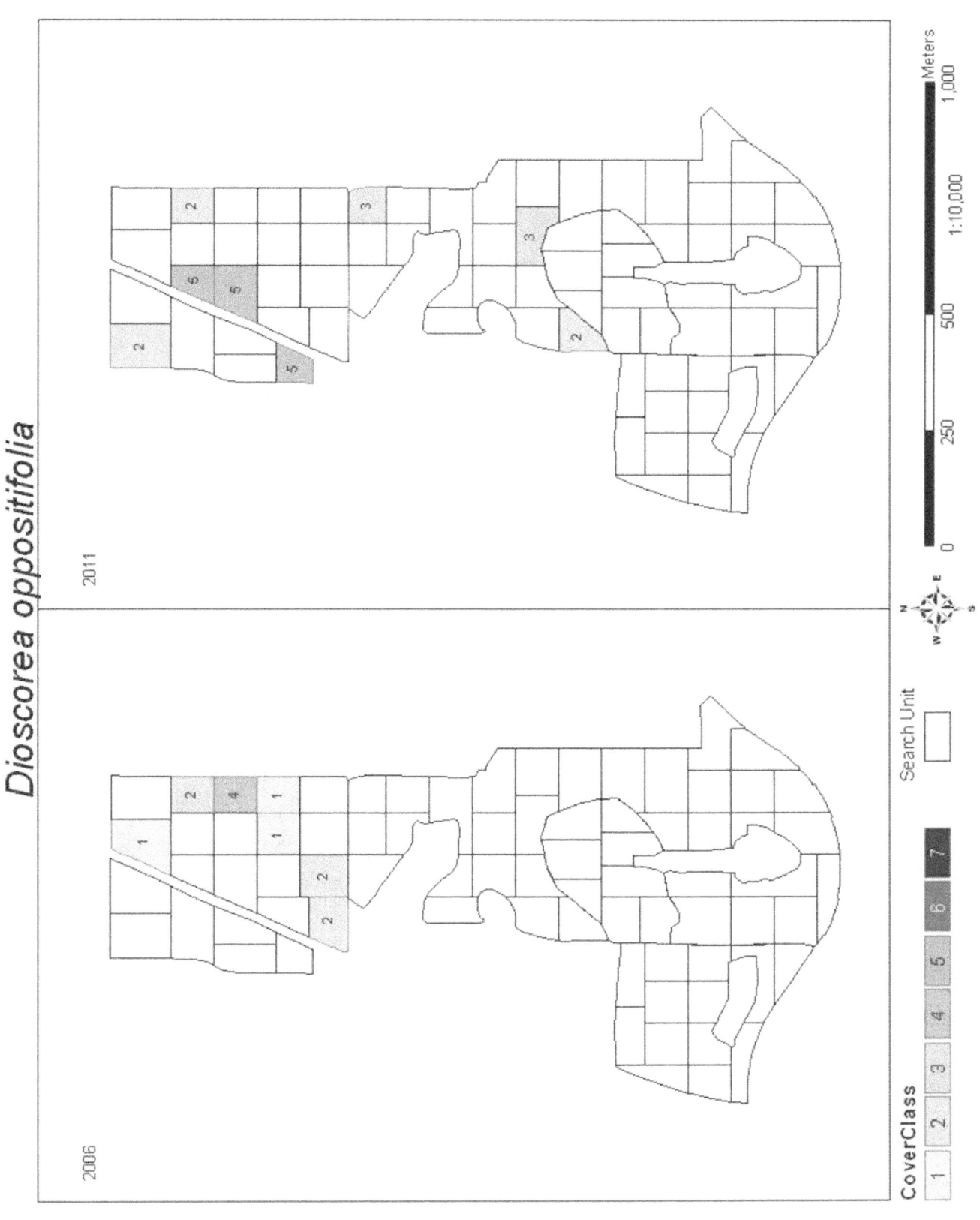

Figure 10. Abundance and distribution of *Dioscorea oppositifolia* (Chinese yam) at Lincoln Boyhood National Memorial, 2006 and 2011. Cover classes are as follows: 1=0.1-0.9 m², 2=1-9.9 m², 3=10-49.9 m², 4= 50-99.9 m², 5=100-499.9 m², 6= 500-999.9 m², 7= 1,000-4,999 m².

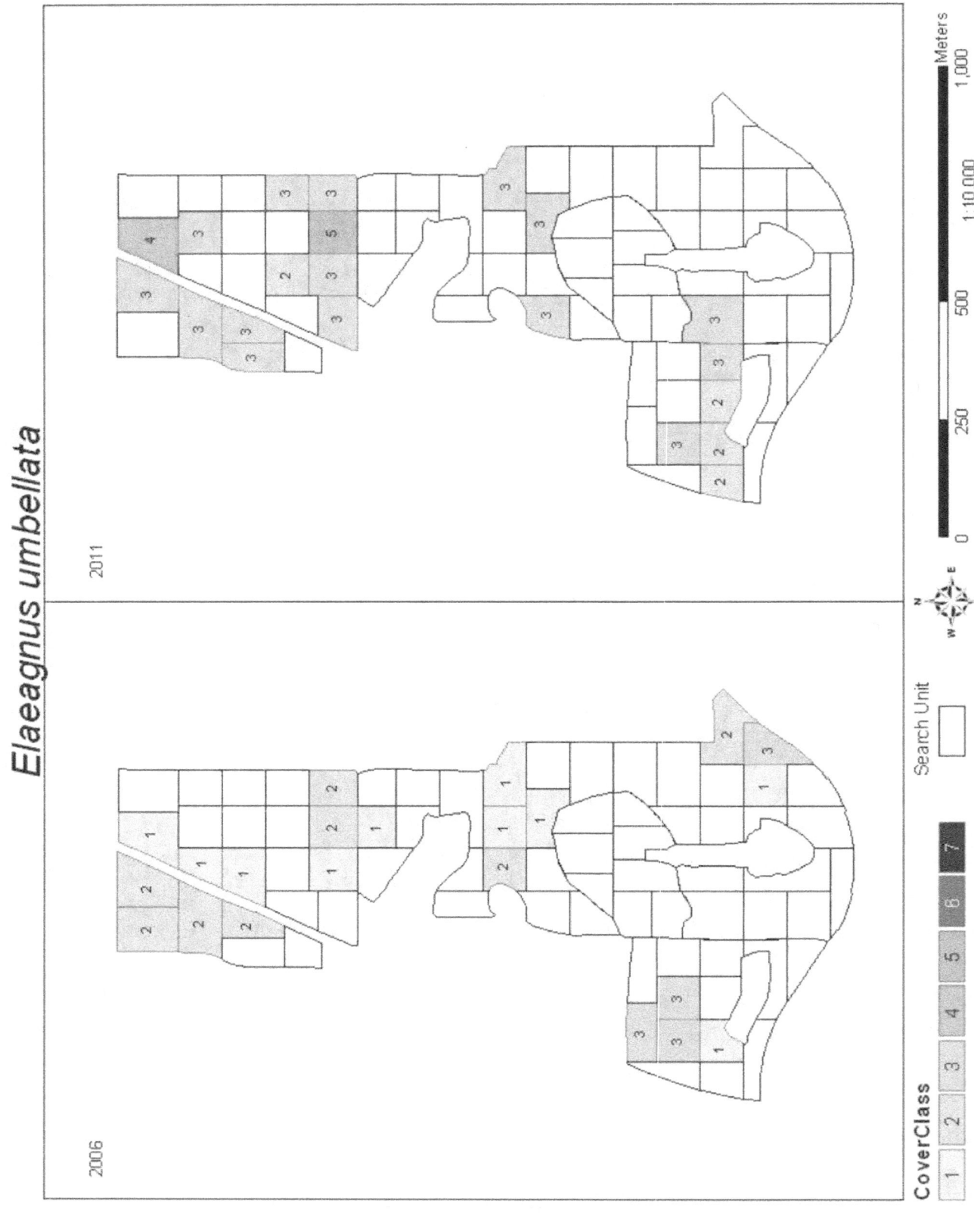

Figure 11. Abundance and distribution of *Elaeagnus umbellata* (autumn olive) at Lincoln Boyhood National Memorial, 2006 and 2011. Cover classes are as follows: $1=0.1-0.9$ m^2, $2=1-9.9$ m^2, $3=10-49.9$ m^2, $4=50-99.9$ m^2, $5=100-499.9$ m^2, $6=500-999.9$ m^2, $7=1,000-4,999$ m^2.

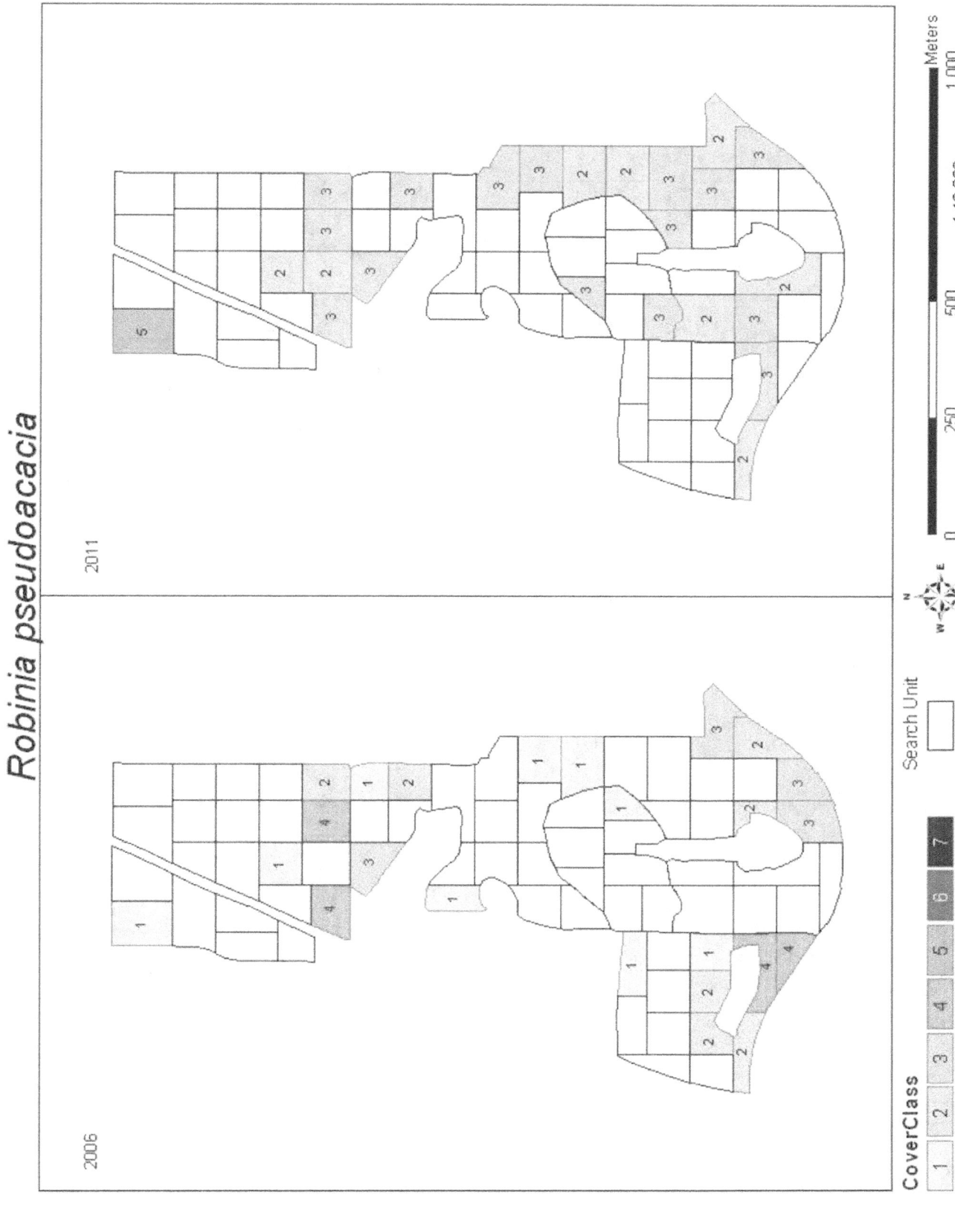

Figure 12. Abundance and distribution of *Robinia pseudoacacia* (black locust) at Lincoln Boyhood National Memorial, 2006 and 2011. Cover classes are as follows: 1=0.1-0.9 m^2, 2=1-9.9 m^2, 3=10-49.9 m^2, 4= 50-99.9 m^2, 5=100-499.9 m^2, 6= 500-999.9 m^2, 7= 1,000-4,999 m^2.

Forsythia suspensa

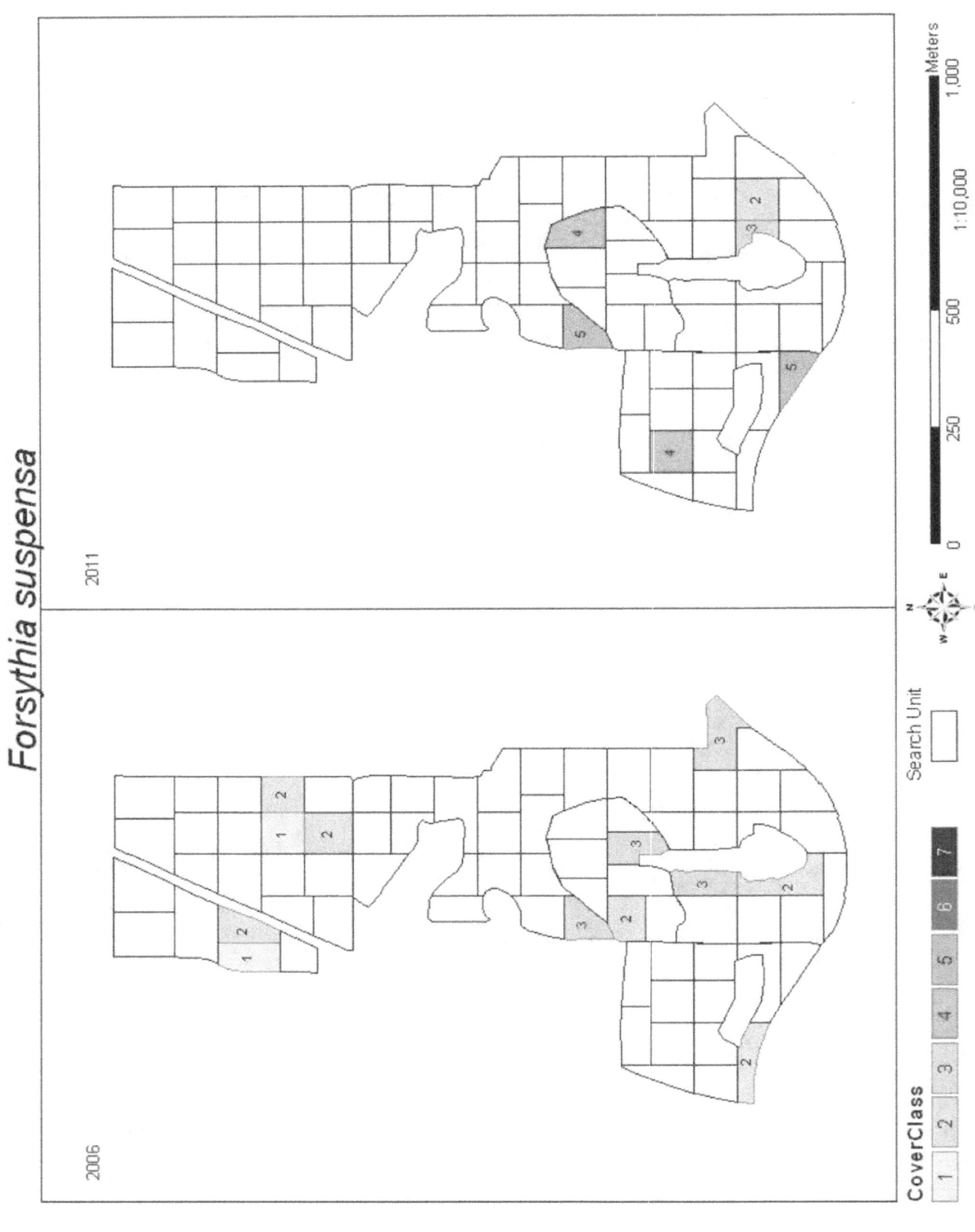

Figure 13. Abundance and distribution of *Forsythia suspensa* (weeping forsythia) at Lincoln Boyhood National Memorial, 2006 and 2011. Cover classes are as follows: 1=0.1-0.9 m^2, 2=1-9.9 m^2, 3=10-49.9 m^2, 4= 50-99.9 m^2, 5=100-499.9 m^2, 6= 500-999.9 m^2, 7= 1,000-4,999 m^2.

Hedera helix

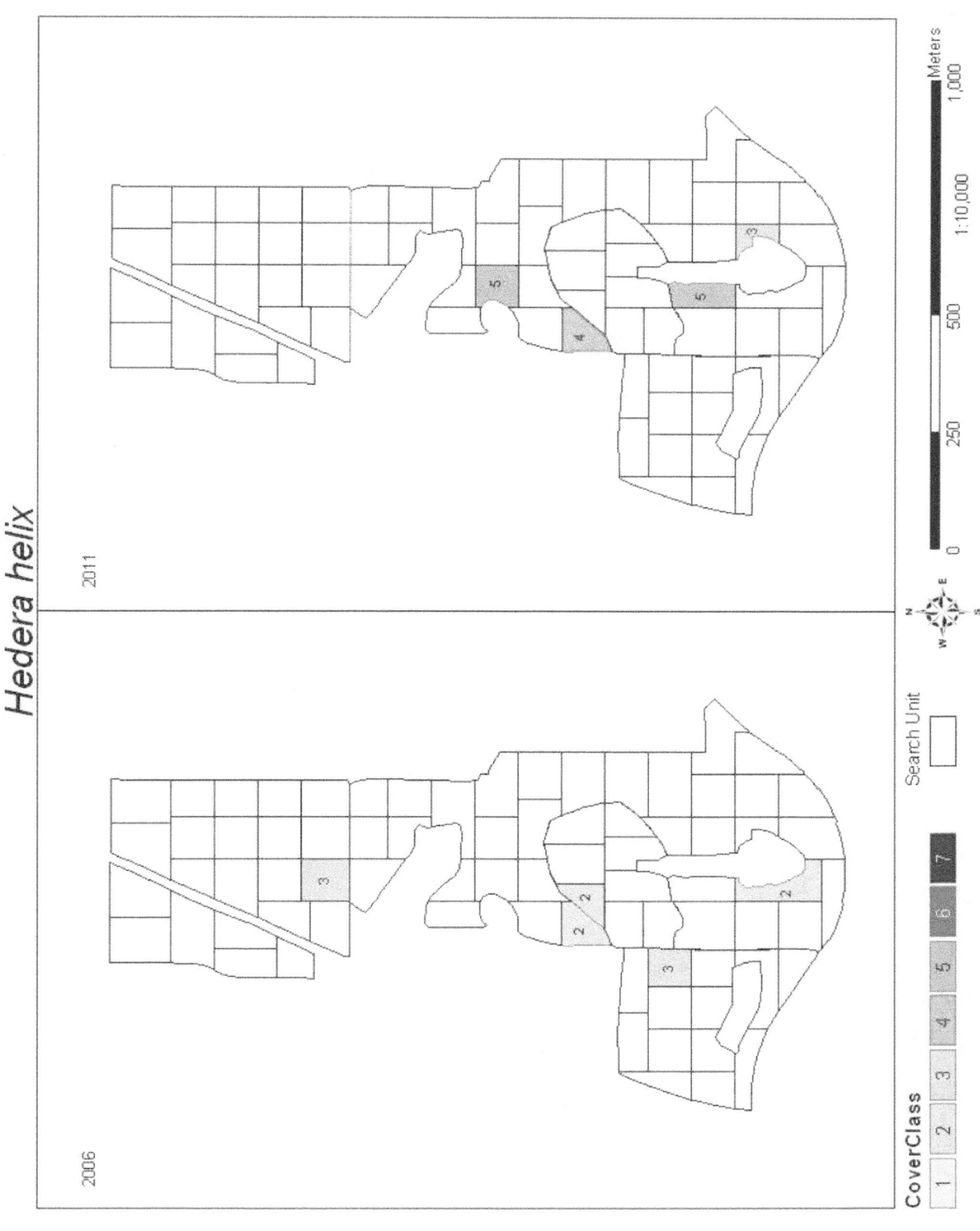

Figure 14. Abundance and distribution of *Hedera helix* (English ivy) at Lincoln Boyhood National Memorial, 2006 and 2011. Cover classes are as follows: 1=0.1-0.9 m^2, 2=1-9.9 m^2, 3=10-49.9 m^2, 4= 50-99.9 m^2, 5=100-499.9 m^2, 6= 500-999.9 m^2, 7= 1,000-4,999 m^2.

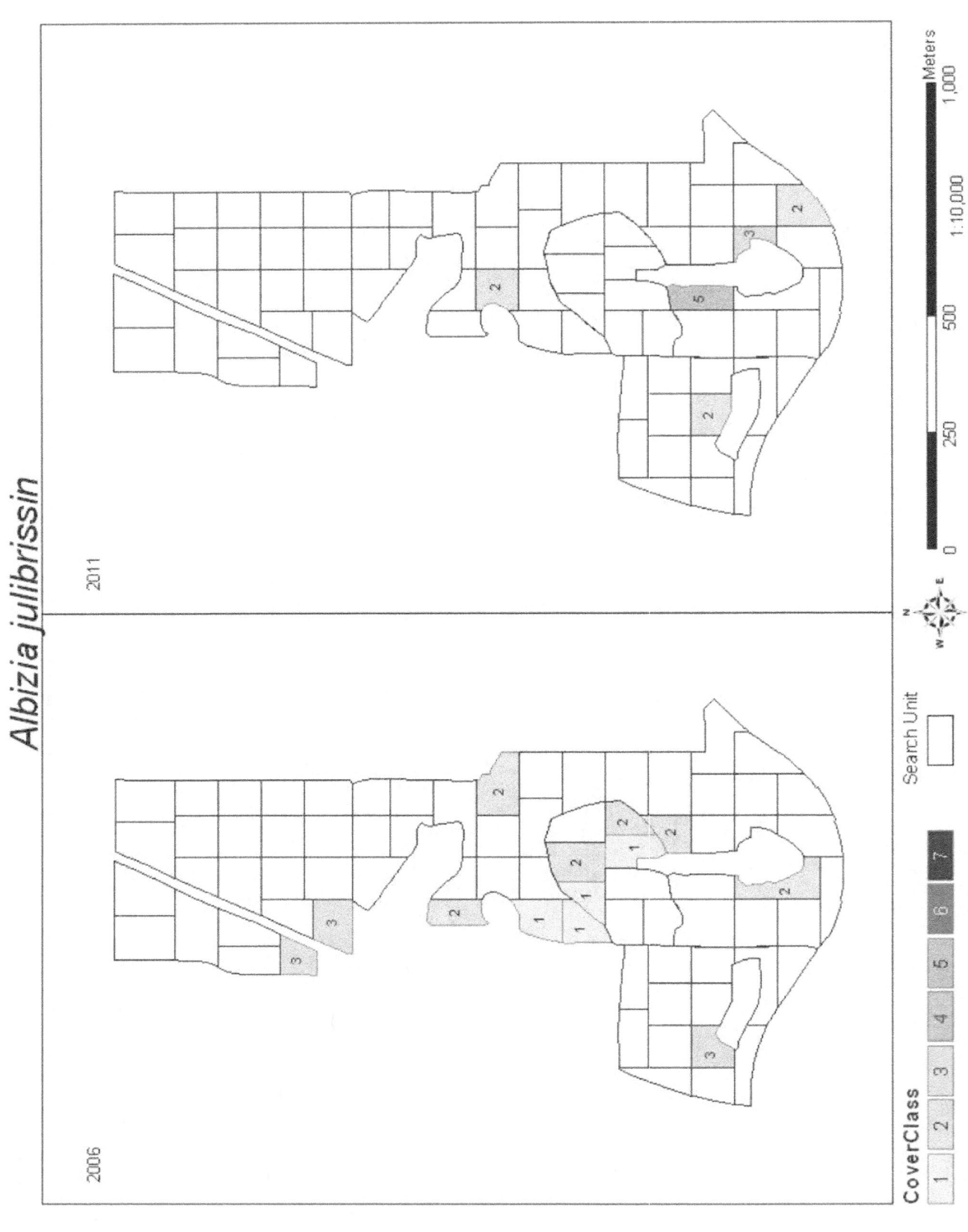

Albizia julibrissin

Figure 15. Abundance and distribution of *Albizia julibrissin* (silktree) at Lincoln Boyhood National Memorial, 2006 and 2011. Cover classes are as follows: 1=0.1-0.9 m², 2=1-9.9 m², 3=10-49.9 m², 4= 50-99.9 m², 5=100-499.9 m², 6= 500-999.9 m², 7= 1,000-4,999 m².

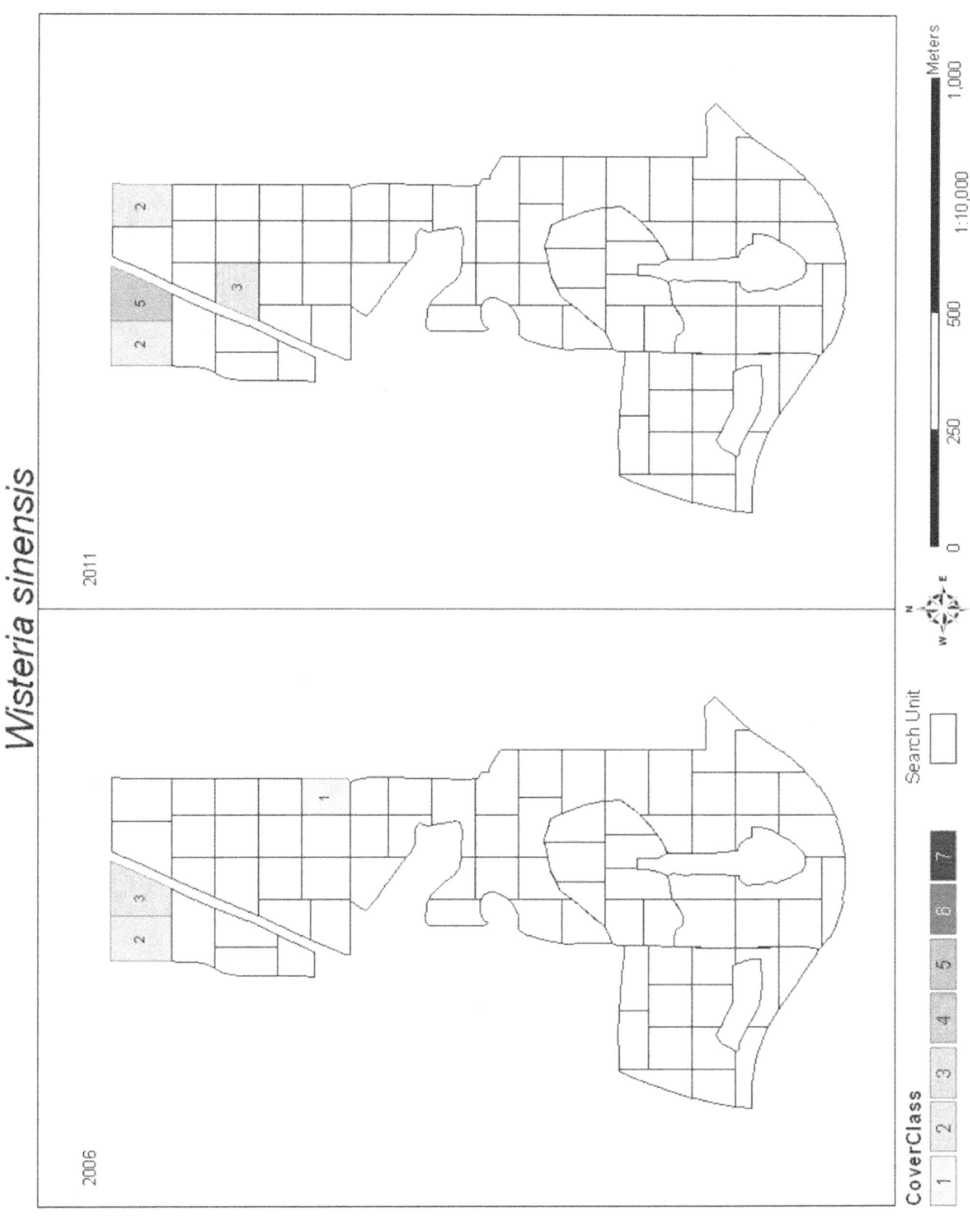

Figure 16. Abundance and distribution of *Wisteria sinensis* (Chinese wisteria) at Lincoln Boyhood National Memorial, 2006 and 2011. Cover classes are as follows: 1=0.1-0.9 m², 2=1-9.9 m², 3=10-49.9 m², 4= 50-99.9 m², 5=100-499.9 m², 6= 500-999.9 m², 7= 1,000-4,999 m².

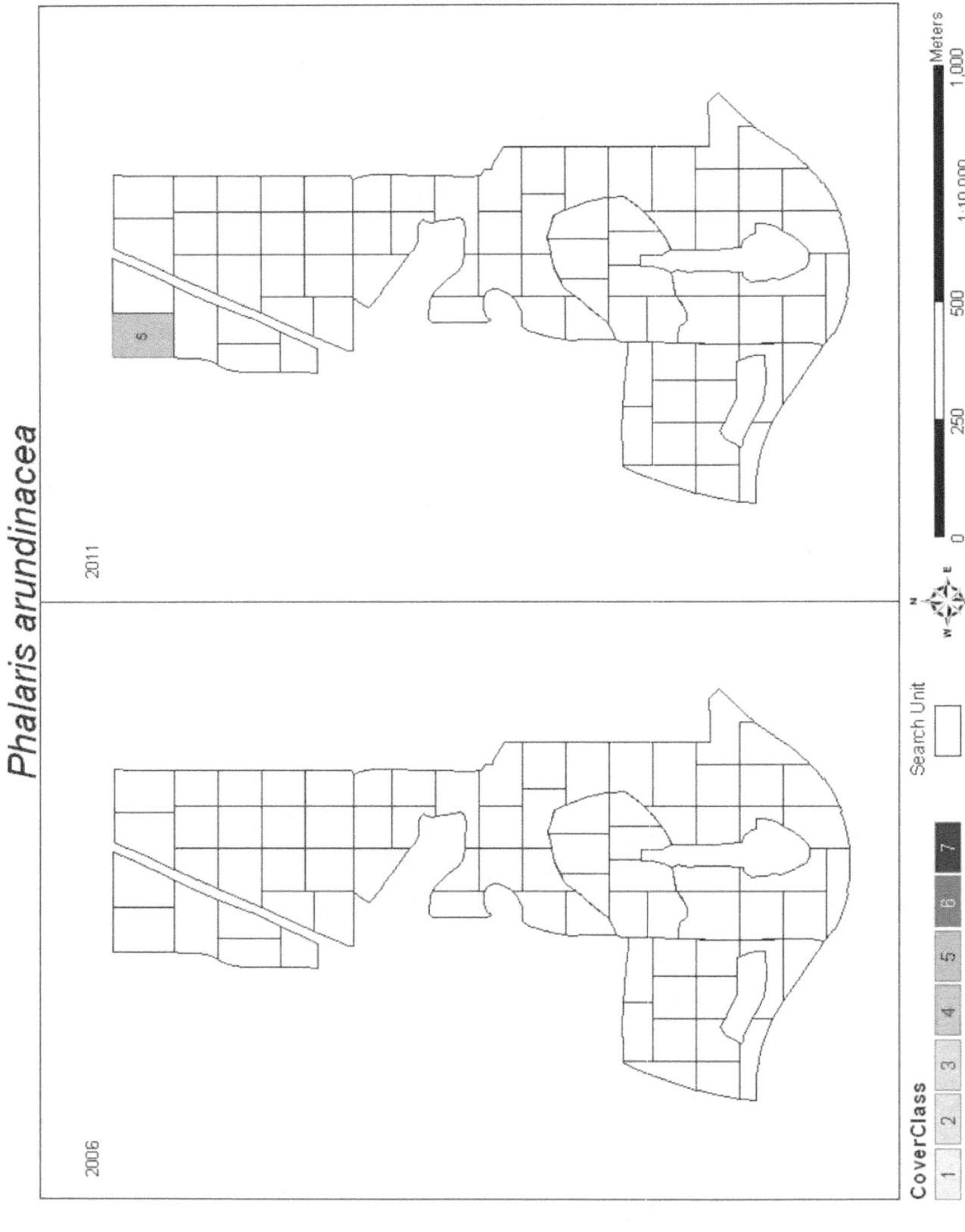

Figure 17. Abundance and distribution of *Phalaris arundinacea* (reed canarygrass) at Lincoln Boyhood National Memorial, 2006 and 2011. Cover classes are as follows: 1=0.1-0.9 m², 2=1-9.9 m², 3=10-49.9 m², 4= 50-99.9 m², 5=100-499.9 m², 6= 500-999.9 m², 7= 1,000-4,999 m².

Ailanthus altissima

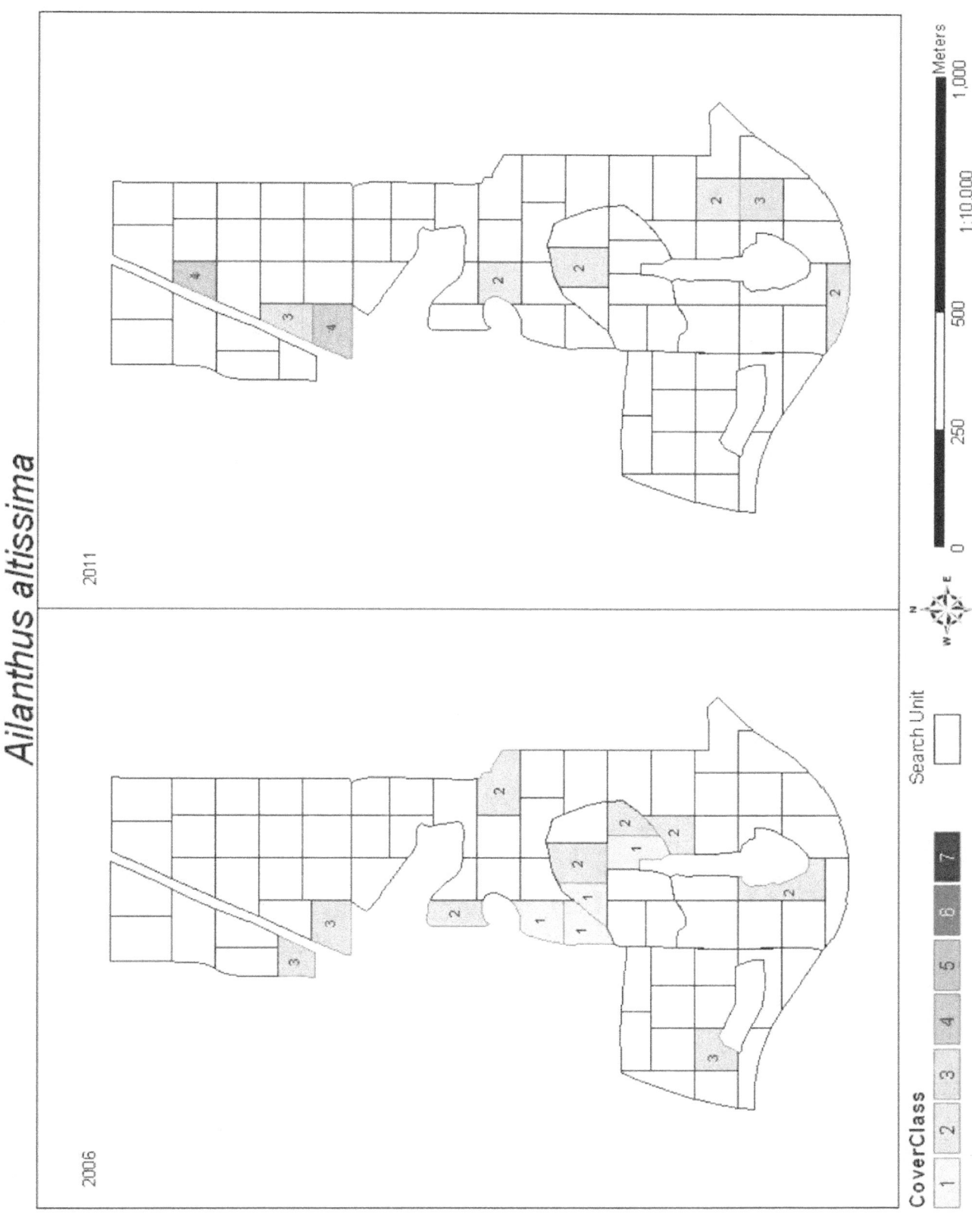

Figure **18**. Abundance and distribution of *Ailanthus altissima* (tree-of-heaven) at Lincoln Boyhood National Memorial, 2006 and 2011. Cover classes are as follows: 1=0.1-0.9 m², 2=1-9.9 m², 3=10-49.9 m², 4= 50-99.9 m², 5=100-499.9 m², 6= 500-999.9 m², 7= 1,000-4,999 m².

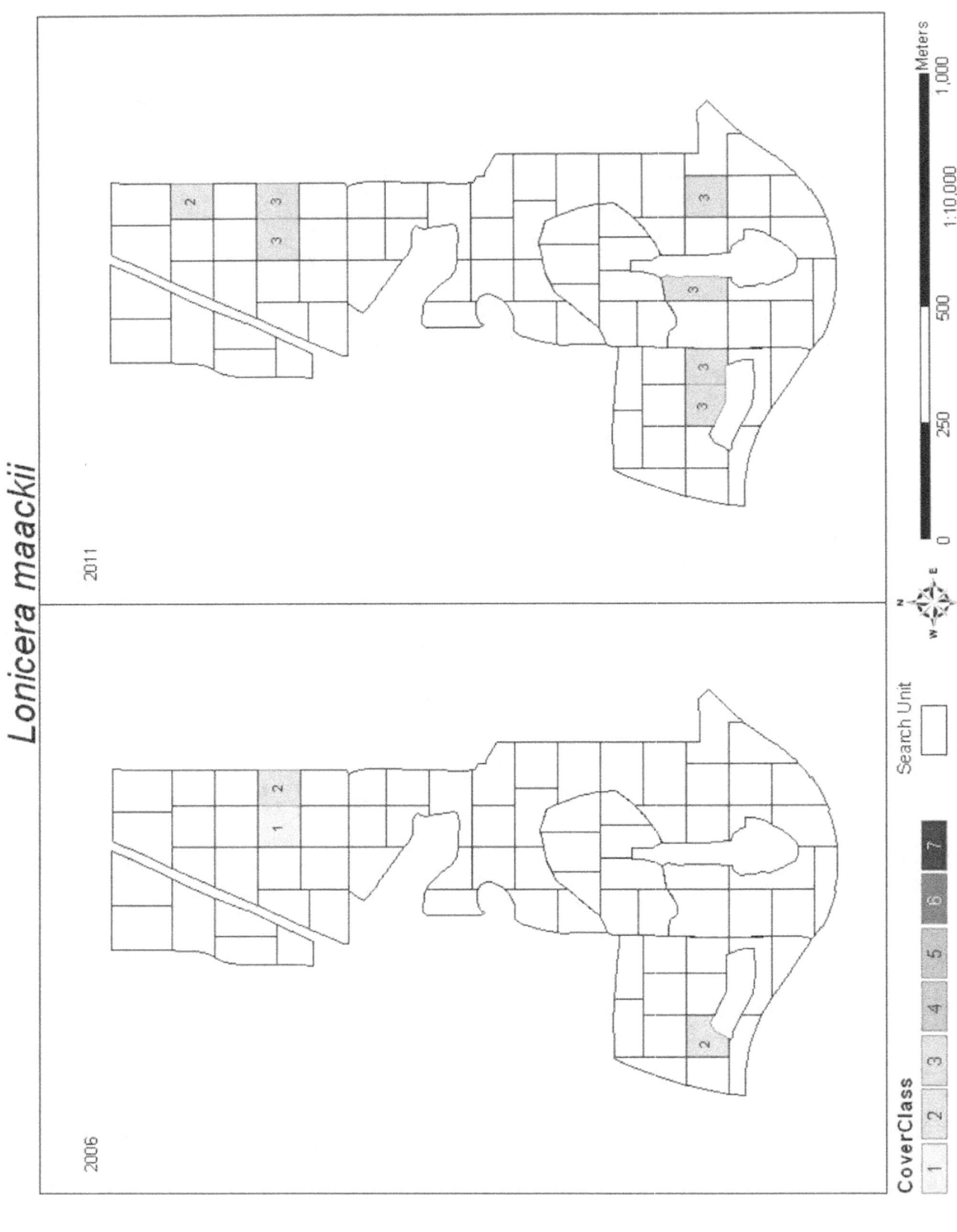

Figure 19. Abundance and distribution of *Lonicera maackii* (amur honeysuckle) at Lincoln Boyhood National Memorial, 2006 and 2011. Cover classes are as follows: 1=0.1-0.9 m², 2=1-9.9 m², 3=10-49.9 m², 4= 50-99.9 m², 5=100-499.9 m², 6= 500-999.9 m², 7= 1,000-4,999 m².

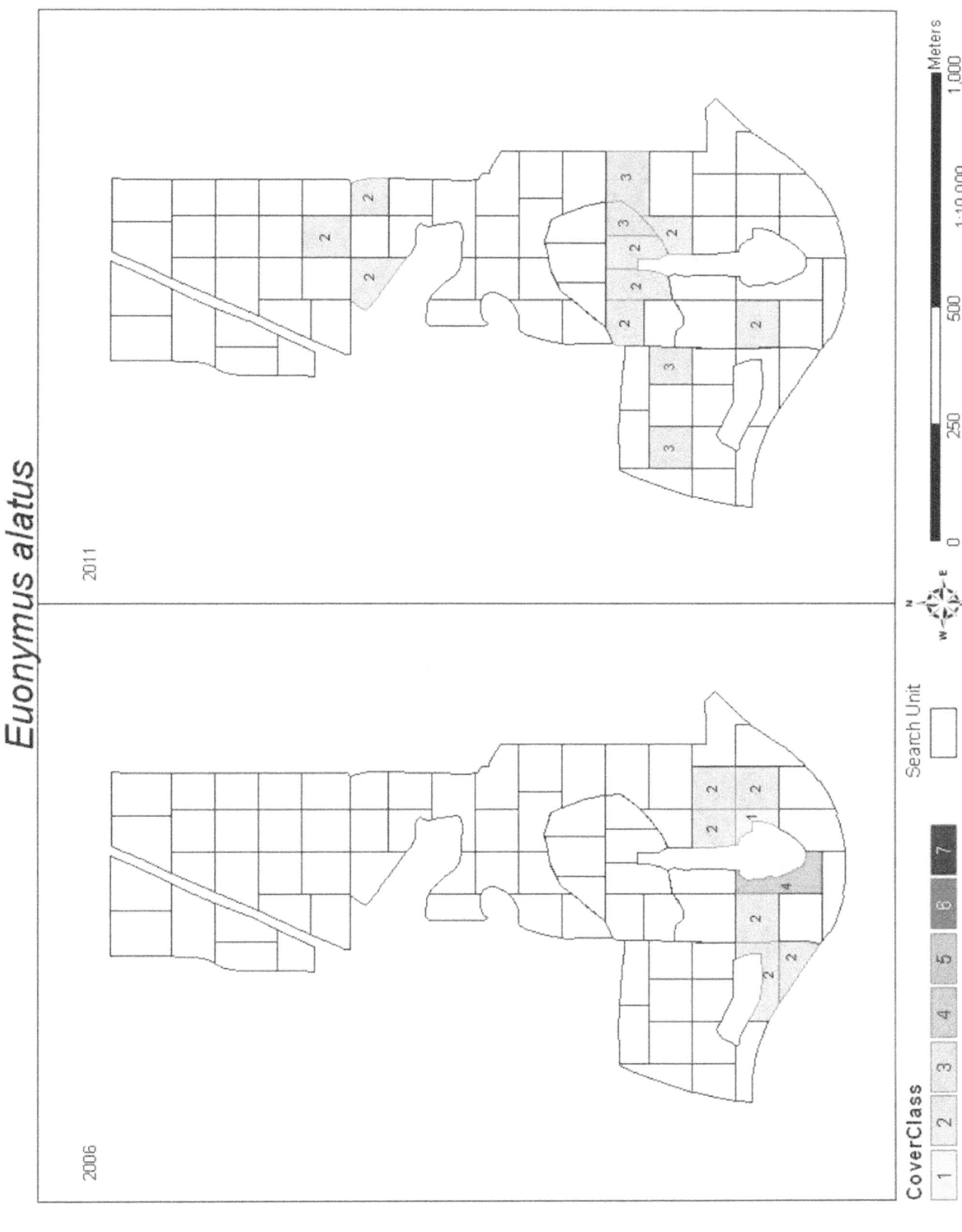

Figure 20. Abundance and distribution of *Euonymus alatus* (winged burningbush) at Lincoln Boyhood National Memorial, 2006 and 2011. Cover classes are as follows: 1=0.1-0.9 m^2, 2=1-9.9 m^2, 3=10-49.9 m^2, 4= 50-99.9 m^2, 5=100-499.9 m^2, 6= 500-999.9 m^2, 7= 1,000-4,999 m^2.

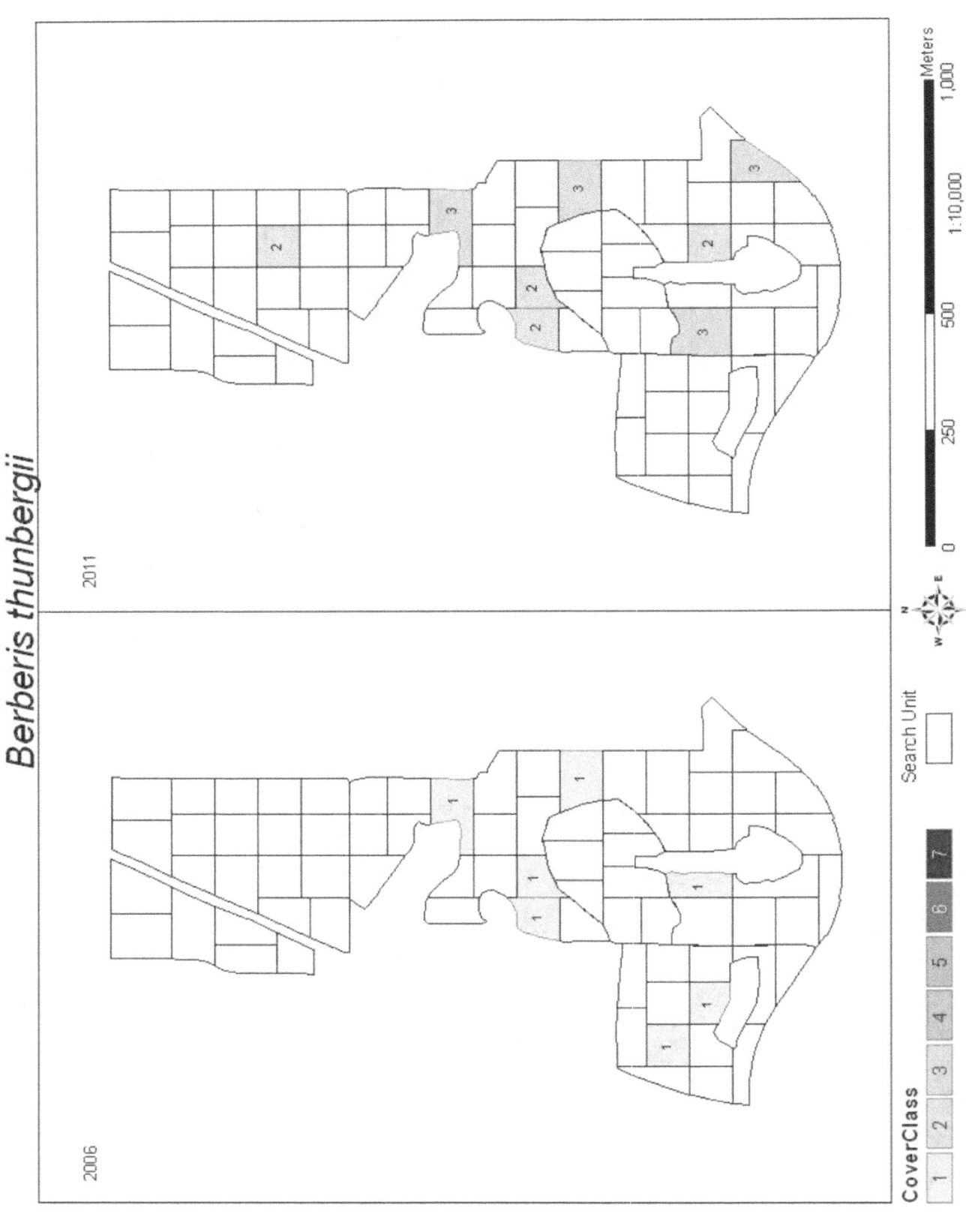

Figure 21. Abundance and distribution of *Berberis thunbergii* (Japanese barberry) at Lincoln Boyhood National Memorial, 2006 and 2011. Cover classes are as follows: 1=0.1-0.9 m², 2=1-9.9 m², 3=10-49.9 m², 4= 50-99.9 m², 5=100-499.9 m², 6= 500-999.9 m², 7= 1,000-4,999 m².

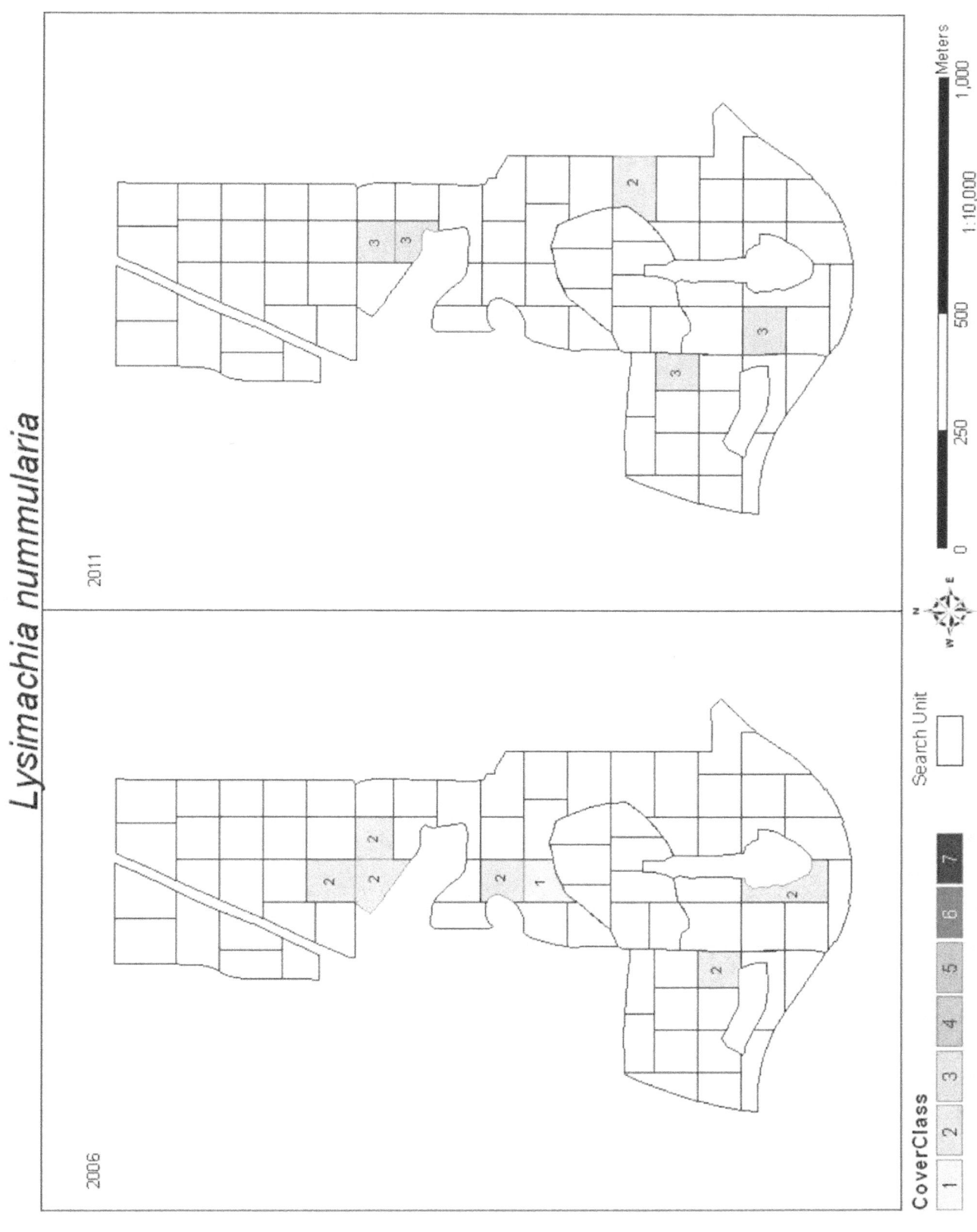

Figure 22. Abundance and distribution of *Lysimachia nummularia* (creeping jenny) at Lincoln Boyhood National Memorial, 2006 and 2011. Cover classes are as follows: 1=0.1-0.9 m^2, 2=1-9.9 m^2, 3=10-49.9 m^2, 4= 50-99.9 m^2, 5=100-499.9 m^2, 6= 500-999.9 m^2, 7= 1,000-4,999 m^2.

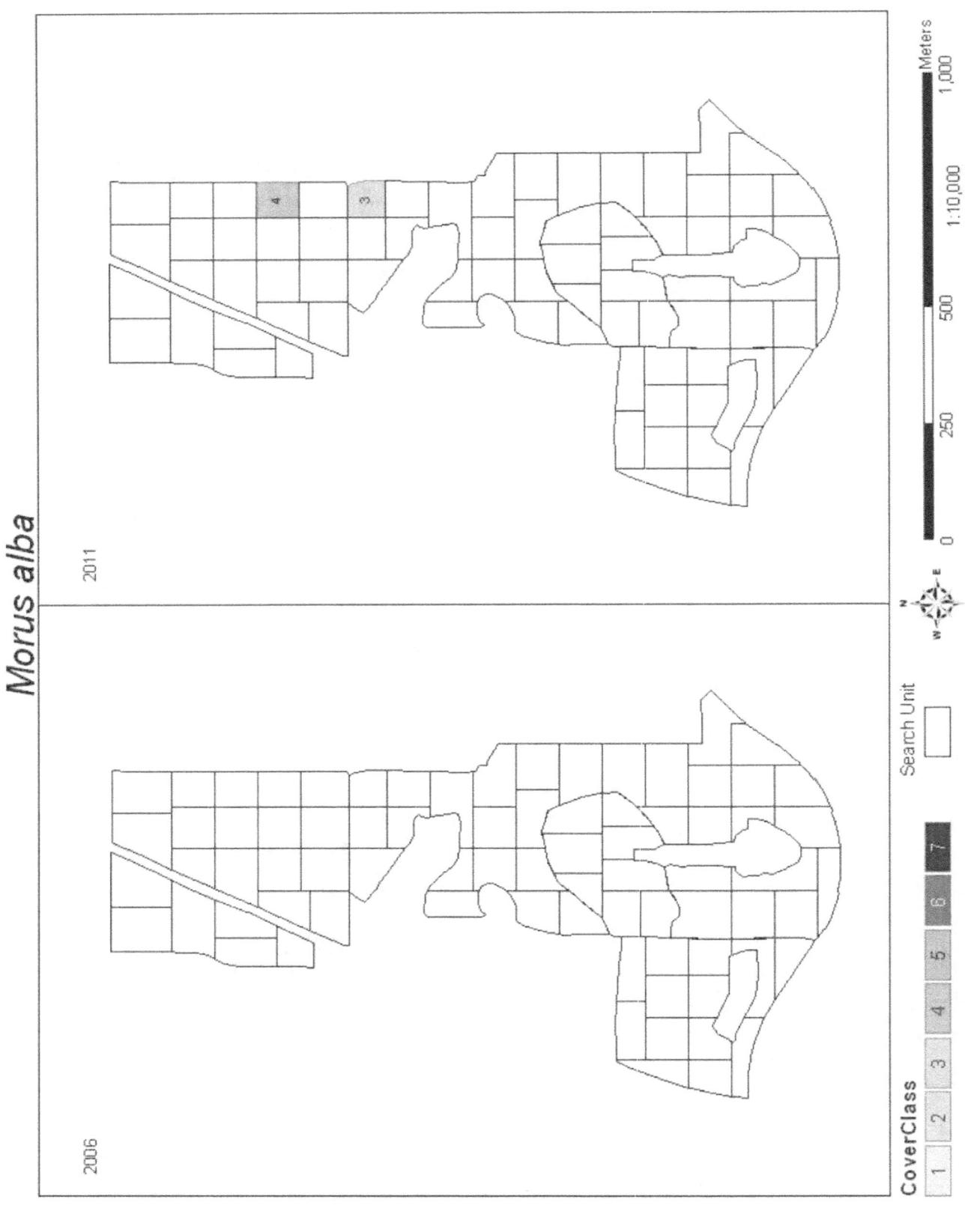

Figure 23. Abundance and distribution of *Morus alba* (white mulberry) at Lincoln Boyhood National Memorial, 2006 and 2011. Cover classes are as follows: 1=0.1-0.9 m^2, 2=1-9.9 m^2, 3=10-49.9 m^2, 4= 50-99.9 m^2, 5=100-499.9 m^2, 6= 500-999.9 m^2, 7= 1,000-4,999 m^2.

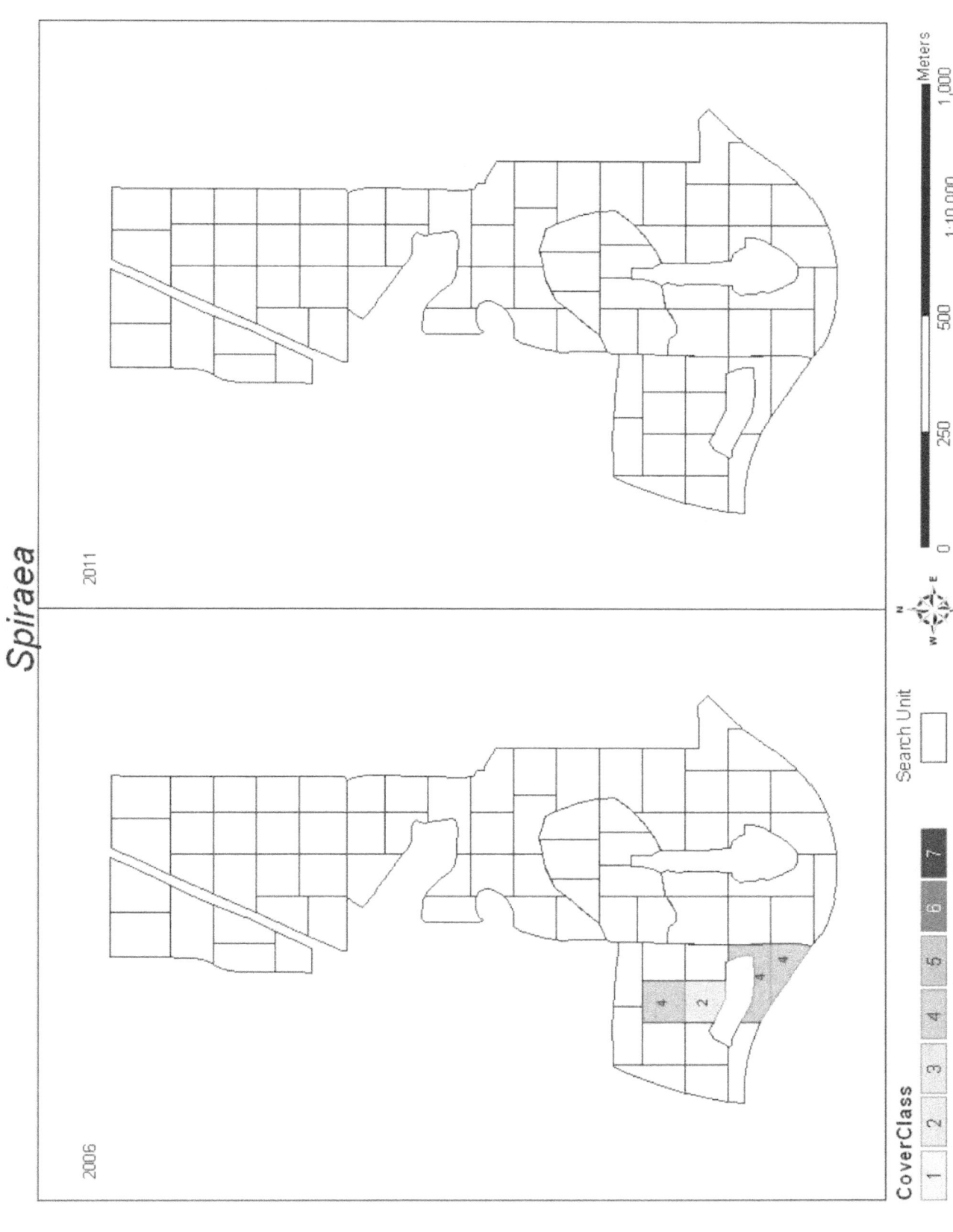

Figure 24. Abundance and distribution of *Spiraea* (*japonica?*) (Japanese spiraea) at Lincoln Boyhood National Memorial, 2006 and 2011. Cover classes are as follows: 1=0.1-0.9 m², 2=1-9.9 m², 3=10-49.9 m², 4= 50-99.9 m², 5=100-499.9 m², 6= 500-999.9 m², 7= 1,000-4,999 m².

Celastrus orbiculatus

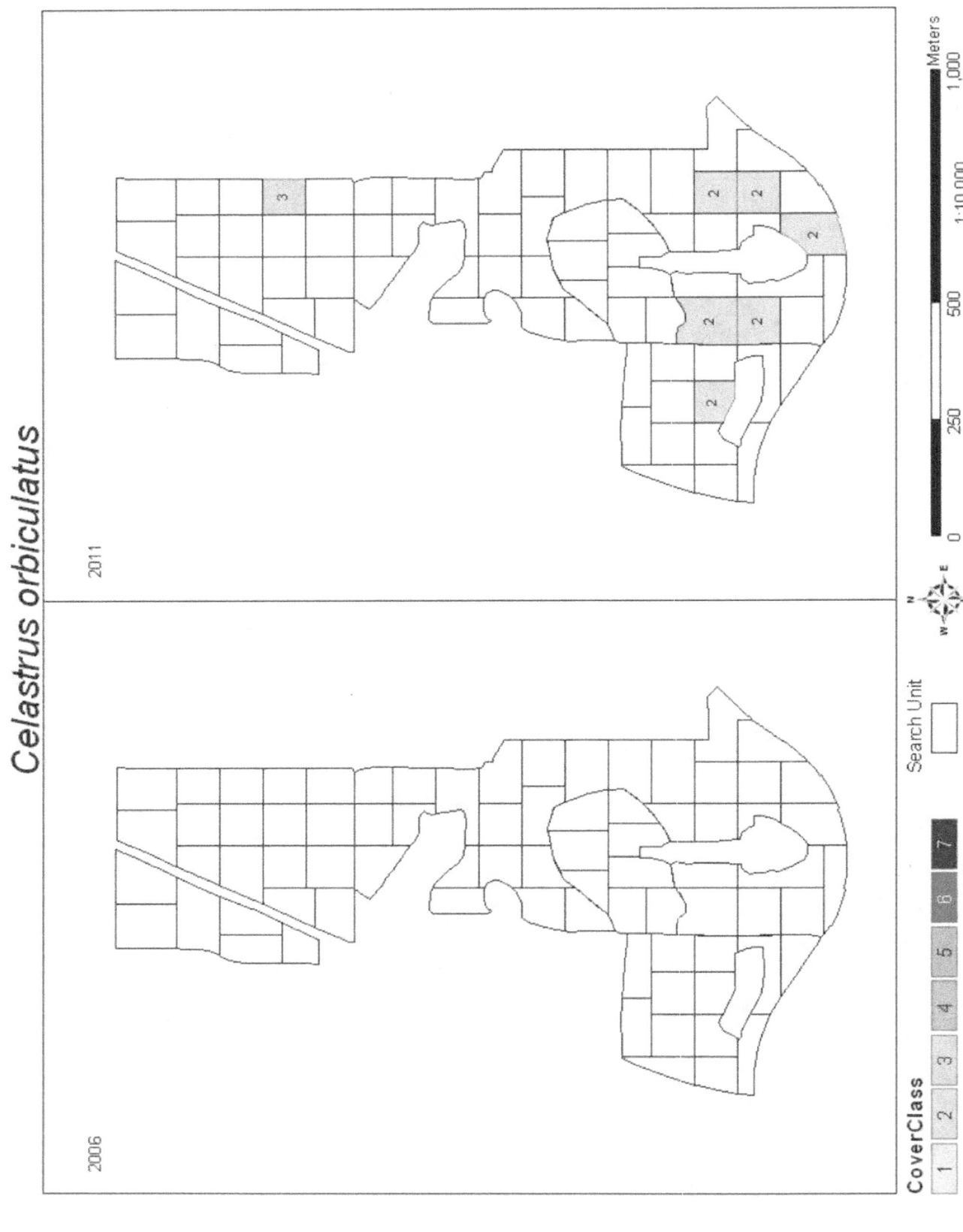

2006

2011

CoverClass

1 | 2 | 3 | 4 | 5 | 6 | 7

Search Unit

N
W E
S

0   250   500   1,000
      Meters

1:10,000

Figure 25. Abundance and distribution of *Celastrus oribculatus* (Oriental bittersweet) at Lincoln Boyhood National Memorial, 2006 and 2011. Cover classes are as follows: 1=0.1-0.9 m^2, 2=1-9.9 m^2, 3=10-49.9 m^2, 4= 50-99.9 m^2, 5=100-499.9 m^2, 6= 500-999.9 m^2, 7= 1,000-4,999 m^2.

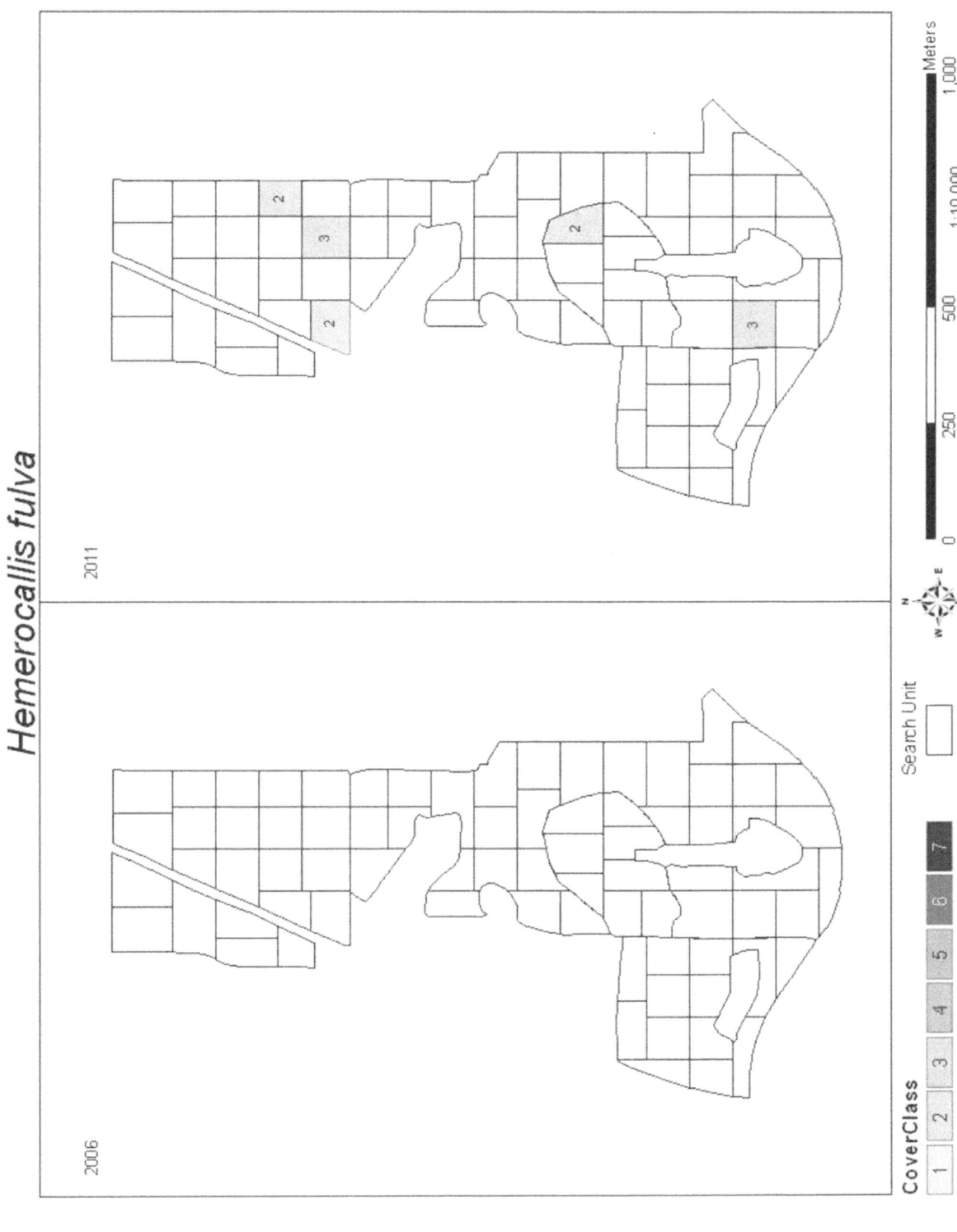

Figure 26. Abundance and distribution of *Hemerocallis fulva* (orange daylily) at Lincoln Boyhood National Memorial, 2006 and 2011. Cover classes are as follows: 1=0.1-0.9 m², 2=1-9.9 m², 3=10-49.9 m², 4= 50-99.9 m², 5=100-499.9 m², 6= 500-999.9 m², 7= 1,000-4,999 m².

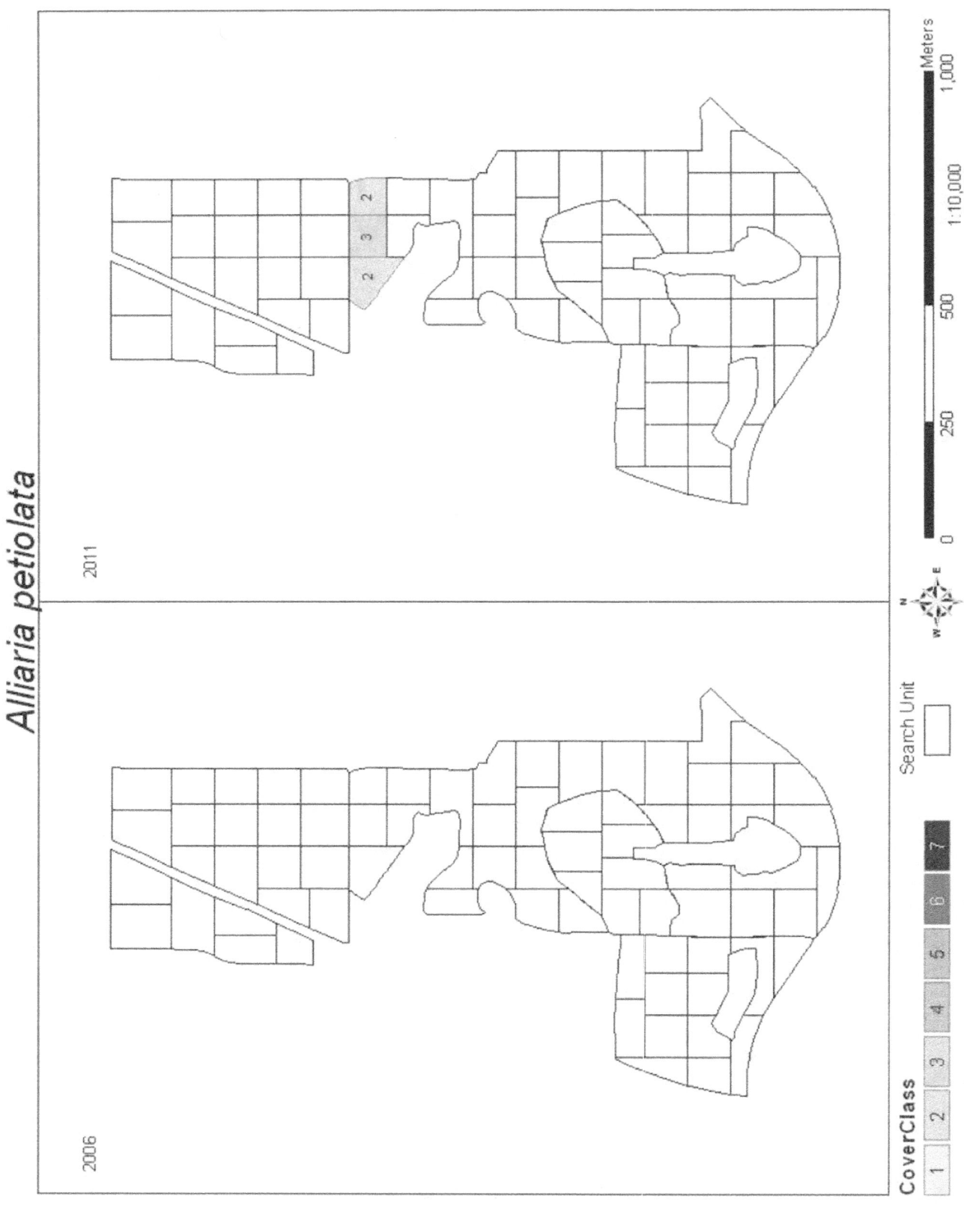

Figure 27. Abundance and distribution of *Alliaria petiolata* (garlic mustard) at Lincoln Boyhood National Memorial, 2006 and 2011. Cover classes are as follows: 1=0.1-0.9 m², 2=1-9.9 m², 3=10-49.9 m², 4= 50-99.9 m², 5=100-499.9 m², 6= 500-999.9 m², 7= 1,000-4,999 m².

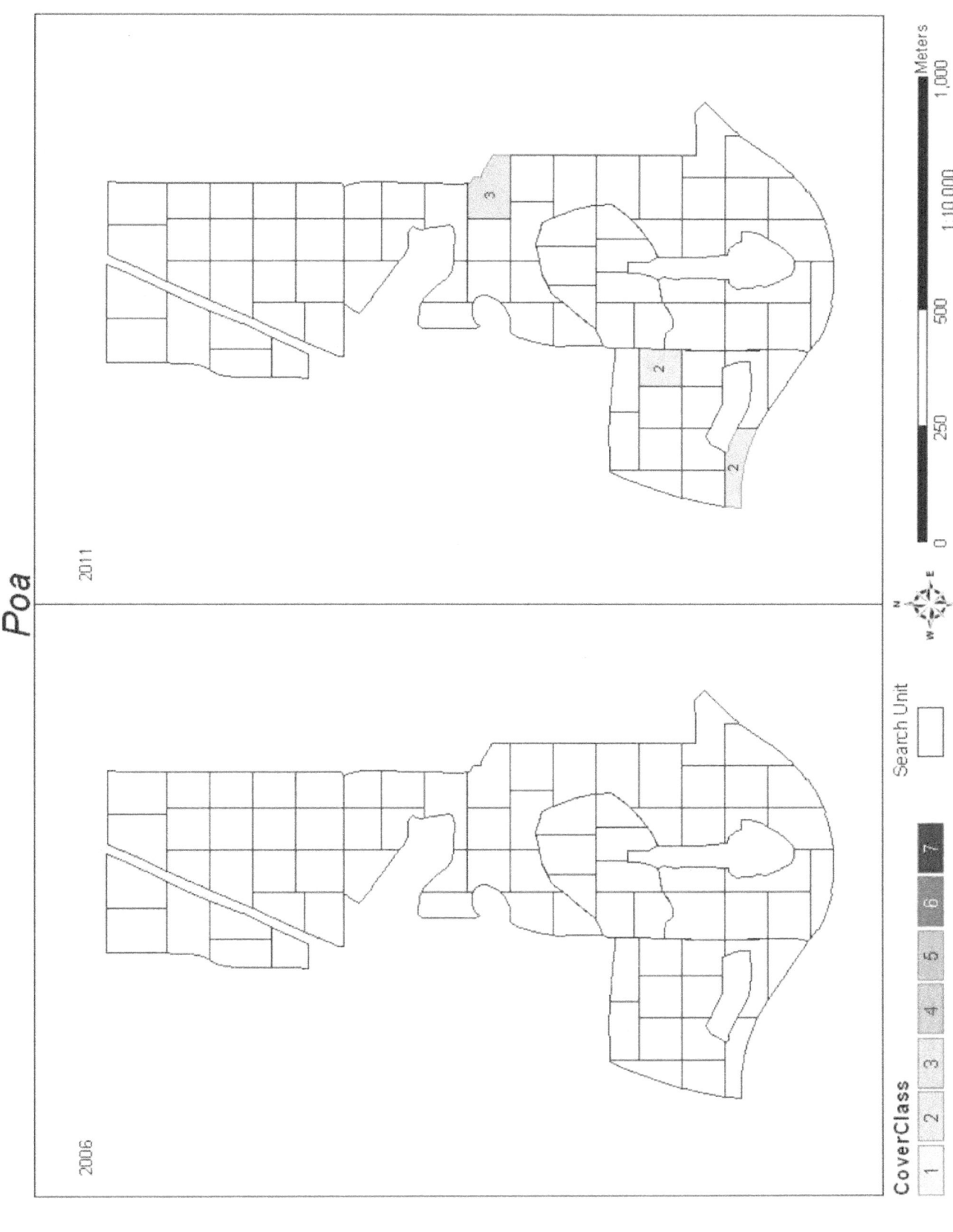

Figure 28. Abundance and distribution of *Poa* (*pratensis?*) (Kentucky bluegrass) at Lincoln Boyhood National Memorial, 2006 and 2011. Cover classes are as follows: 1=0.1-0.9 m², 2=1-9.9 m², 3=10-49.9 m², 4= 50-99.9 m², 5=100-499.9 m², 6= 500-999.9 m², 7= 1,000-4,999 m².

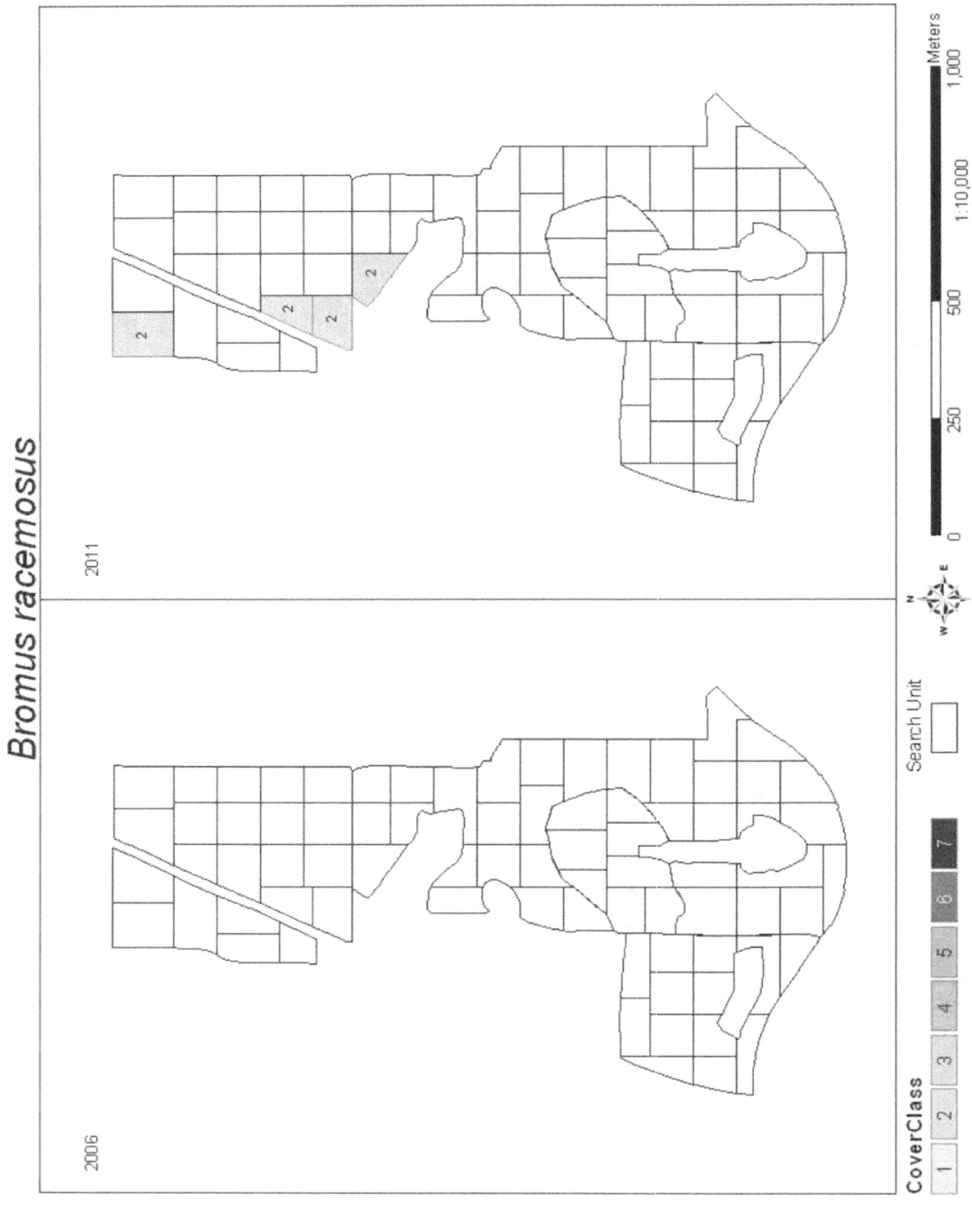

Figure 29. Abundance and distribution of *Bromus racemosus* (bald brome) at Lincoln Boyhood National Memorial, 2006 and 2011. Cover classes are as follows: 1=0.1-0.9 m², 2=1-9.9 m², 3=10-49.9 m², 4= 50-99.9 m², 5=100-499.9 m², 6= 500-999.9 m², 7= 1,000-4,999 m².

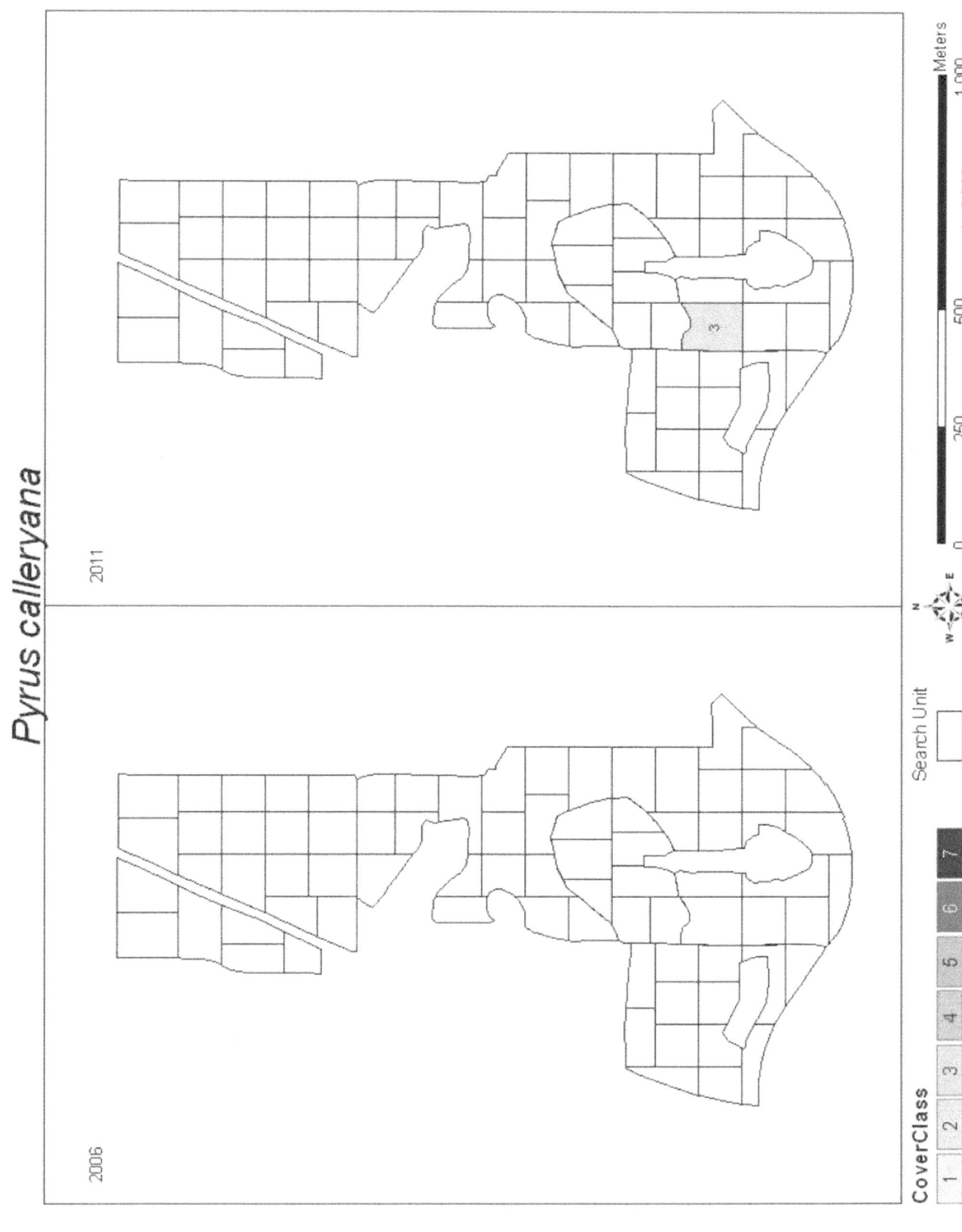

Figure 30. Abundance and distribution of *Pyrus calleryana* (Callery pear) at Lincoln Boyhood National Memorial, 2006 and 2011. Cover classes are as follows: 1=0.1-0.9 m², 2=1-9.9 m², 3=10-49.9 m², 4= 50-99.9 m², 5=100-499.9 m², 6= 500-999.9 m², 7= 1,000-4,999 m².

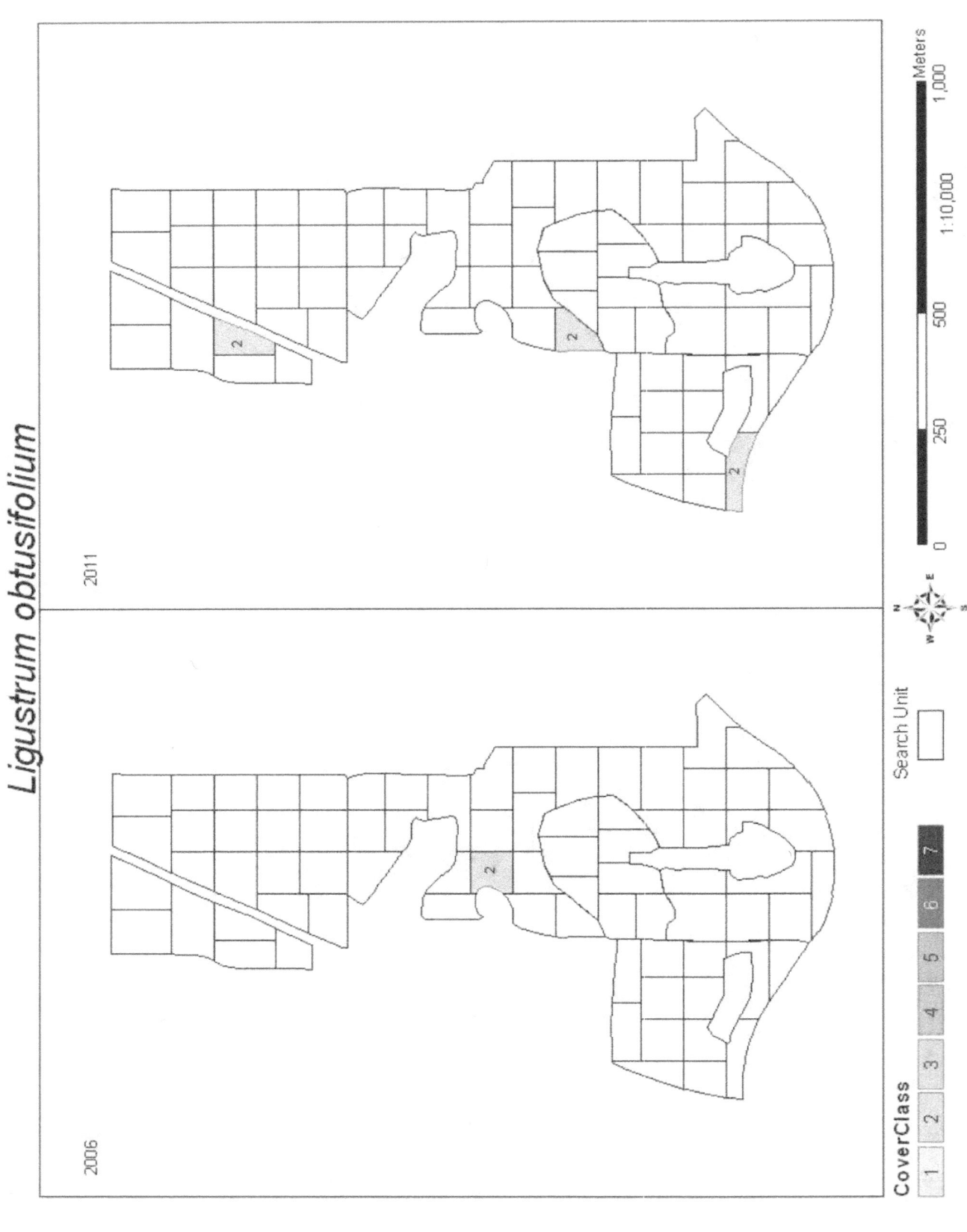

Figure 31. Abundance and distribution of *Ligustrum obtusifolium* (border privet) at Lincoln Boyhood National Memorial, 2006 and 2011. Cover classes are as follows: 1=0.1-0.9 m², 2=1-9.9 m², 3=10-49.9 m², 4= 50-99.9 m², 5=100-499.9 m², 6= 500-999.9 m², 7= 1,000-4,999 m².

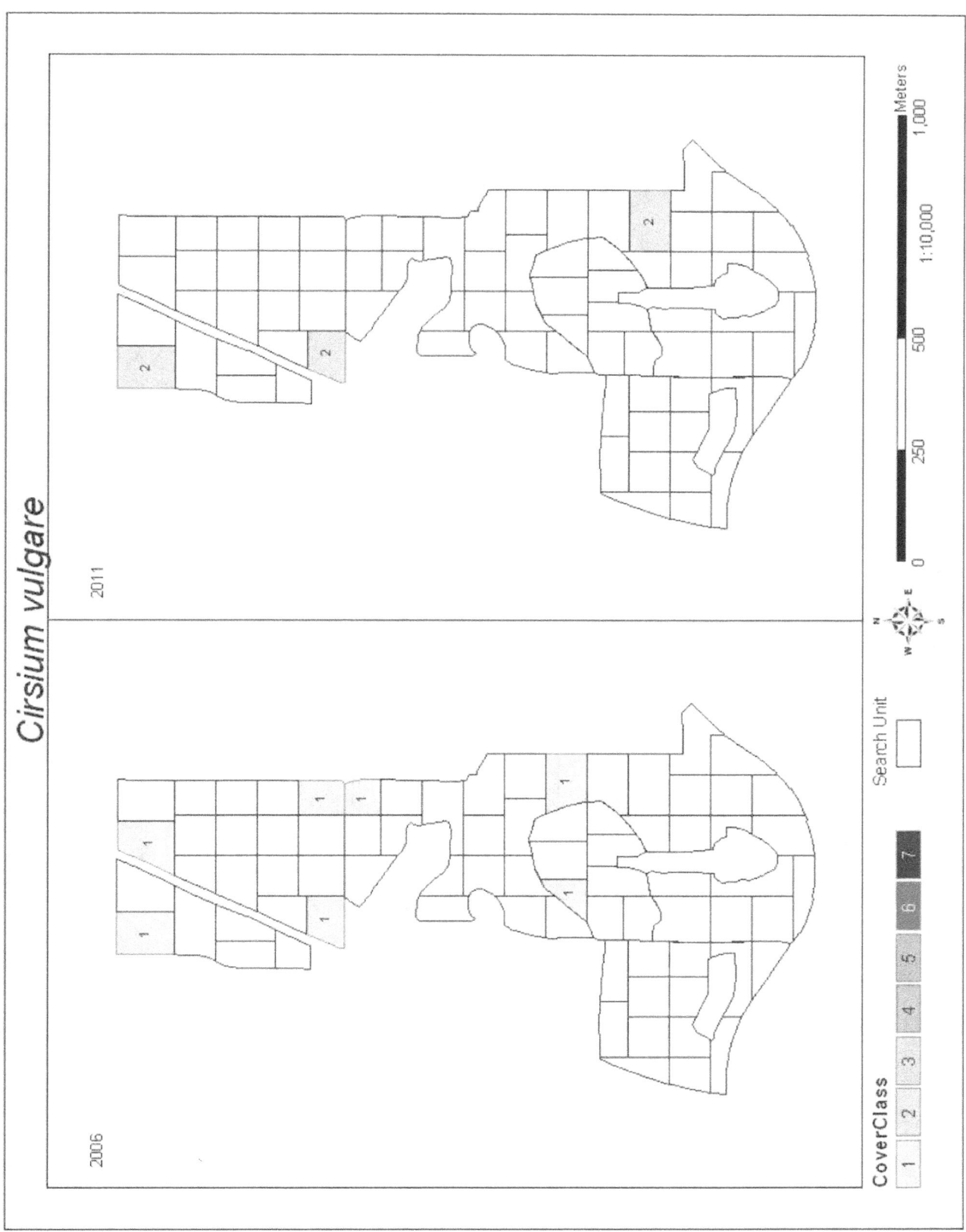

Figure 32. Abundance and distribution of *Cirsium vulgare* (bull thistle) at Lincoln Boyhood National Memorial, 2006 and 2011. Cover classes are as follows: 1=0.1-0.9 m², 2=1-9.9 m², 3=10-49.9 m², 4= 50-99.9 m², 5=100-499.9 m², 6= 500-999.9 m², 7= 1,000-4,999 m².

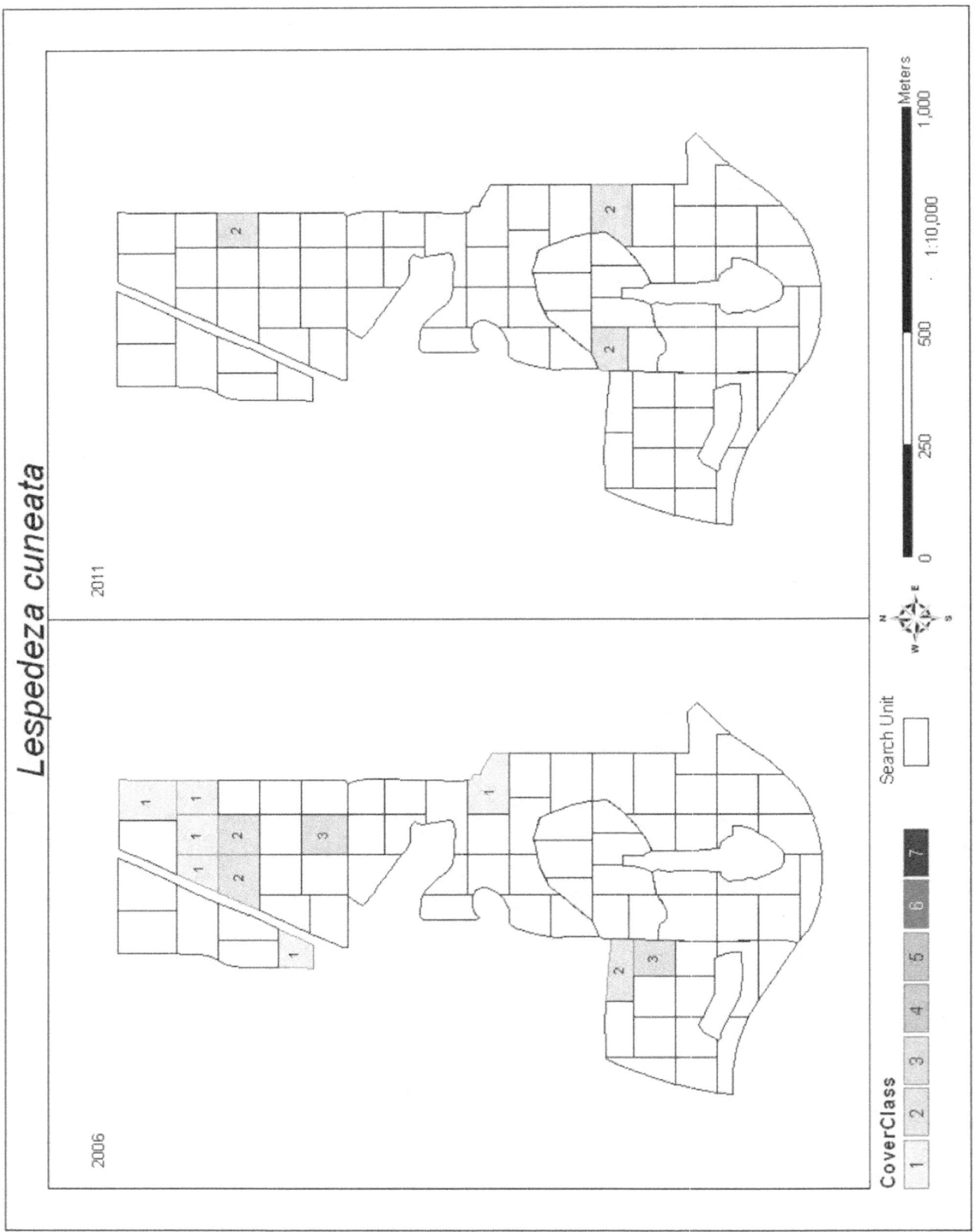

Figure 33. Abundance and distribution of *Lespedeza cuneata* (sericea lespedeza) at Lincoln Boyhood National Memorial, 2006 and 2011. Cover classes are as follows: 1=0. 1-0.9 m^2, 2=1-9.9 m^2, 3=10-49.9 m^2, 4= 50-99.9 m^2, 5=100-499.9 m^2, 6= 500-999.9 m^2, 7= 1,000-4,999 m^2.

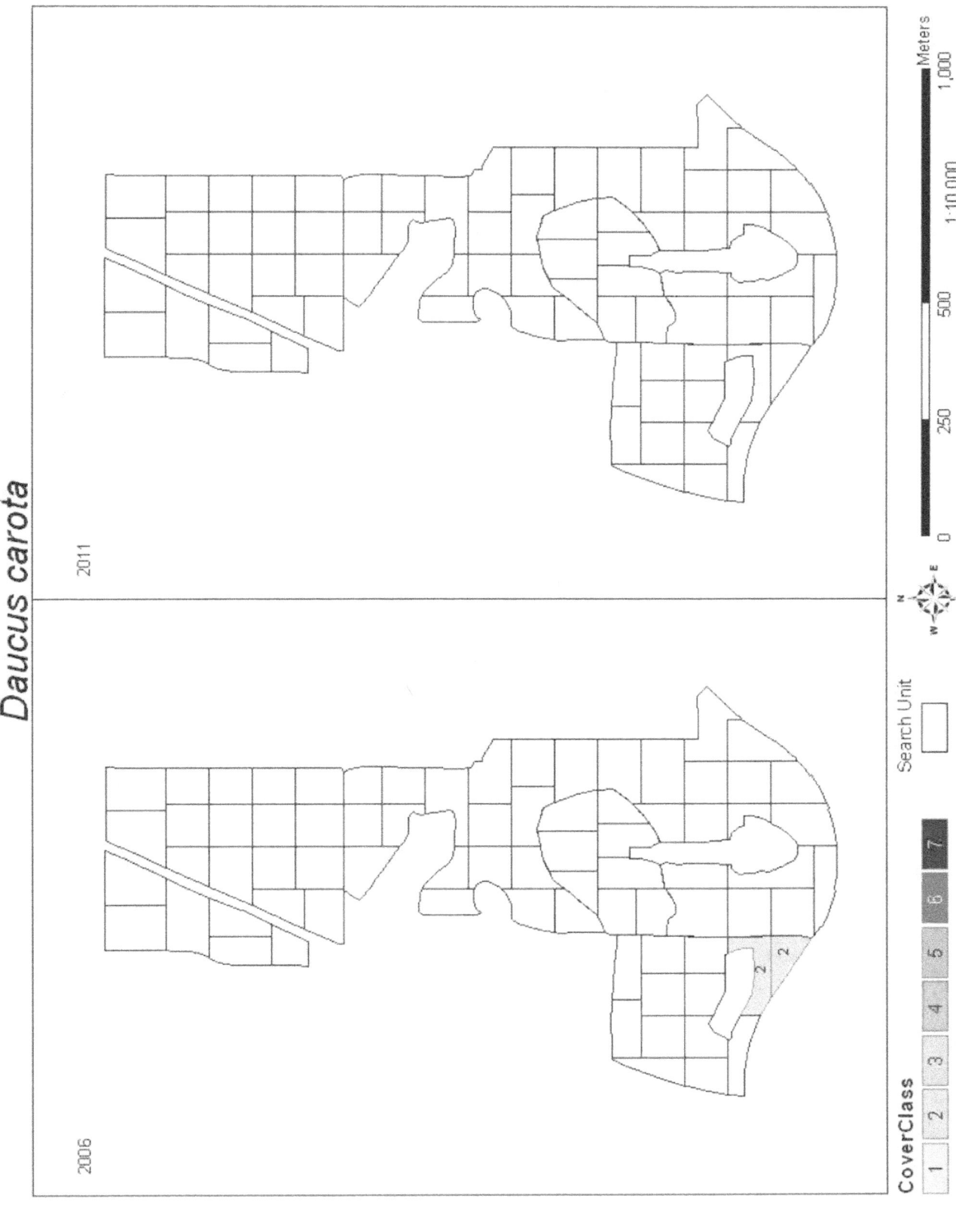

Figure 34. Abundance and distribution of *Daucus carota* (Queen Anne's lace) at Lincoln Boyhood National Memorial, 2006 and 2011. Cover classes are as follows: 1=0.1-0.9 m^2, 2=1-9.9 m^2, 3=10-49.9 m^2, 4= 50-99.9 m^2, 5=100-499.9 m^2, 6= 500-999.9 m^2, 7= 1,000-4,999 m^2.

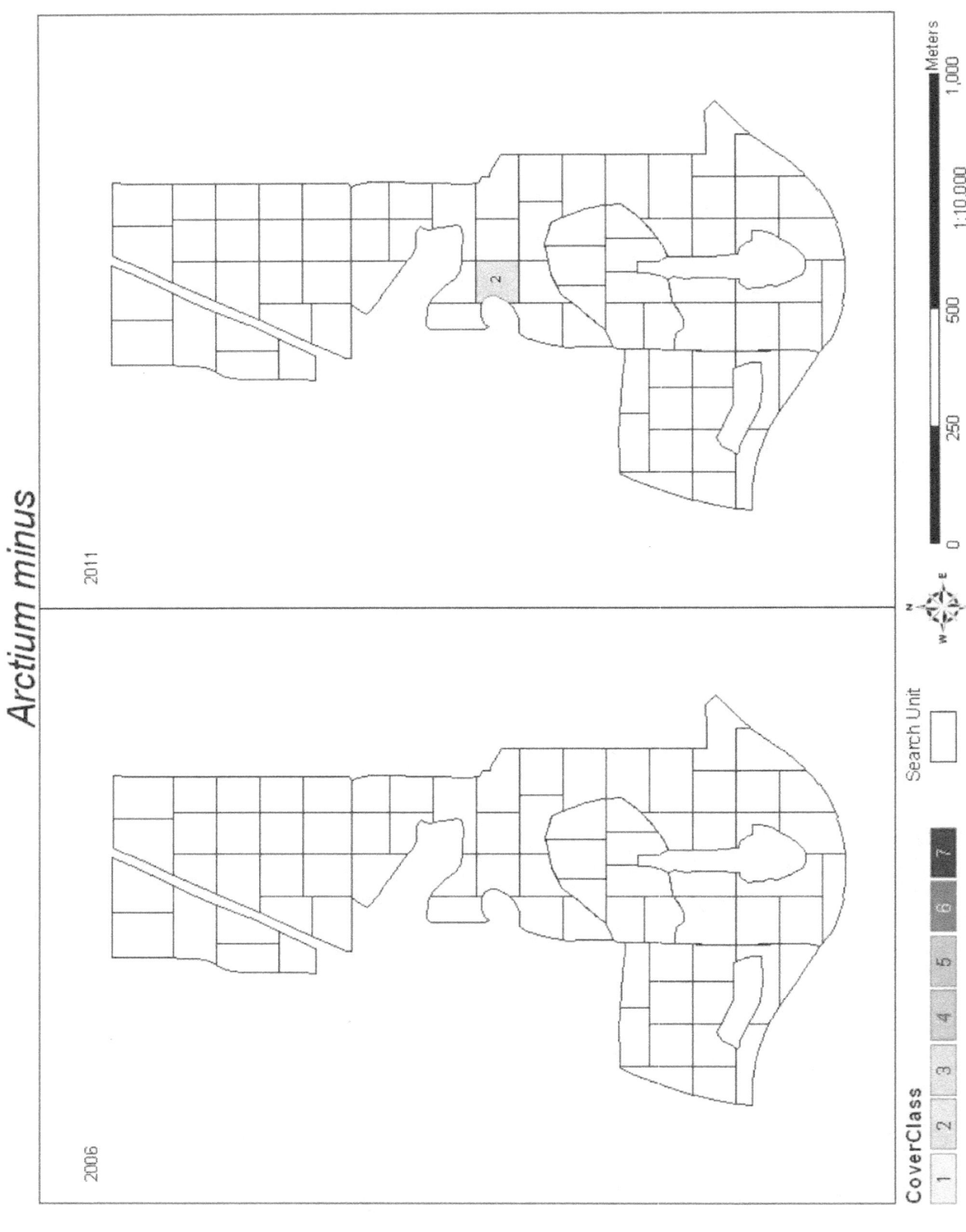

Figure 35. Abundance and distribution of *Arctium minus* (lesser burdock) at Lincoln Boyhood National Memorial, 2006 and 2011. Cover classes are as follows: 1=0.1-0.9 m², 2=1-9.9 m², 3=10-49.9 m², 4= 50-99.9 m², 5=100-499.9 m², 6= 500-999.9 m², 7= 1,000-4,999 m².

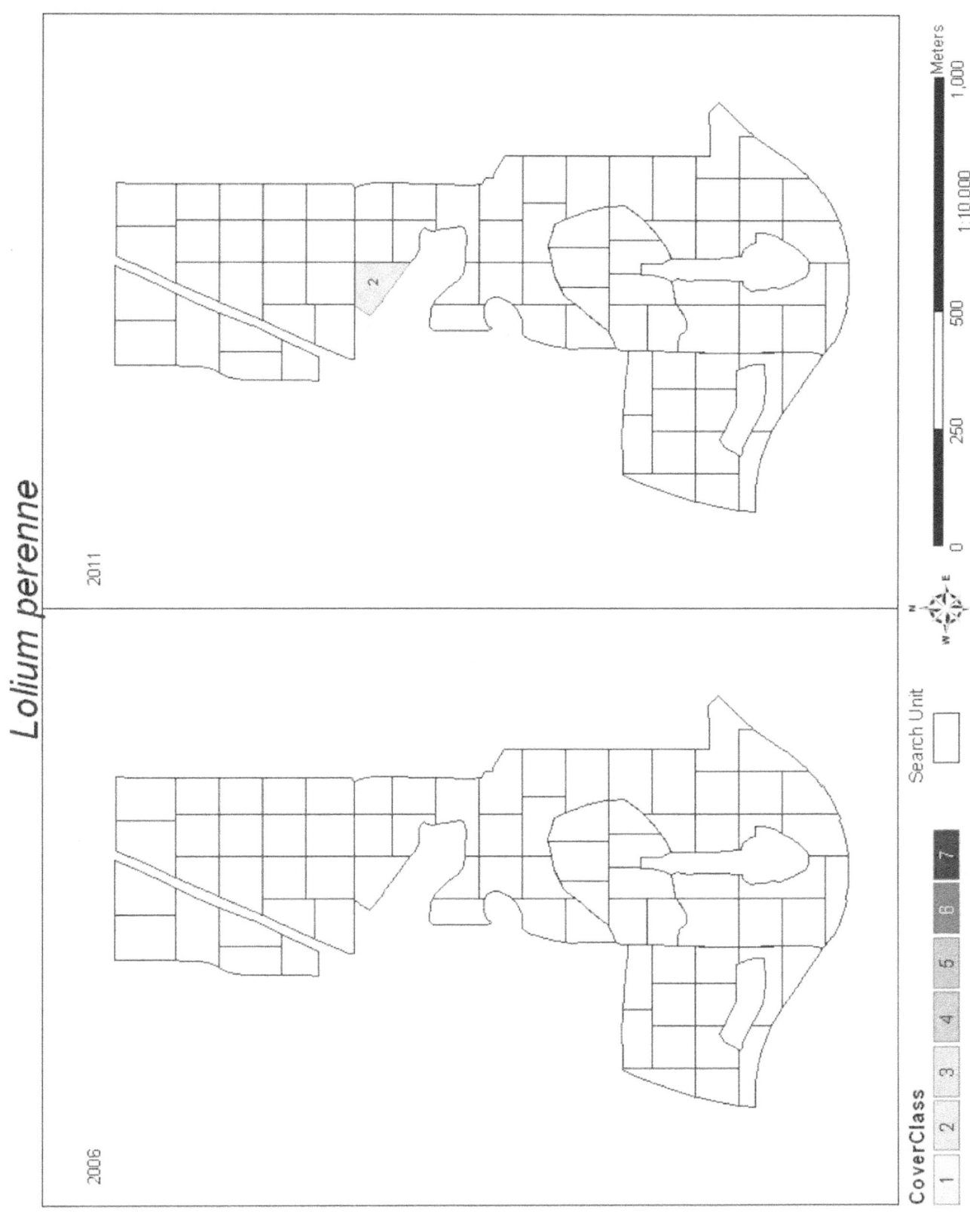

Figure 36. Abundance and distribution of *Loilum perenne* (perennial ryegrass) at Lincoln Boyhood National Memorial, 2006 and 2011. Cover classes are as follows: 1=0.1-0.9 m², 2=1-9.9 m², 3=10-49.9 m², 4= 50-99.9 m², 5=100-499.9 m², 6= 500-999.9 m², 7= 1,000-4,999 m².

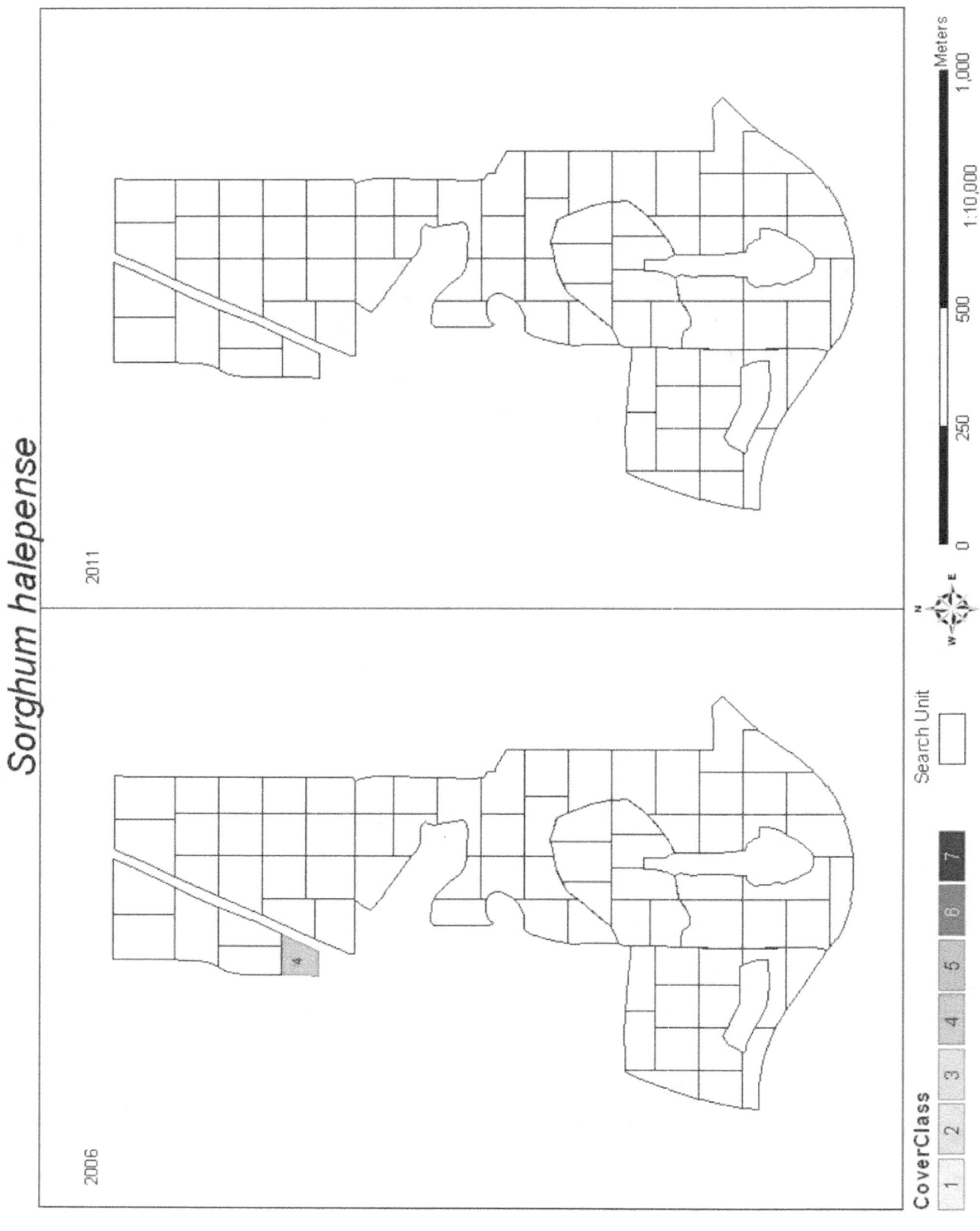

Figure 37. Abundance and distribution of *Sorghum halepense* (Johnsongrass) at Lincoln Boyhood National Memorial, 2006 and 2011. Cover classes are as follows: 1=0.1-0.9 m², 2=1-9.9 m², 3=10-49.9 m², 4= 50-99.9 m², 5=100-499.9 m², 6= 500-999.9 m², 7= 1,000-4,999 m².

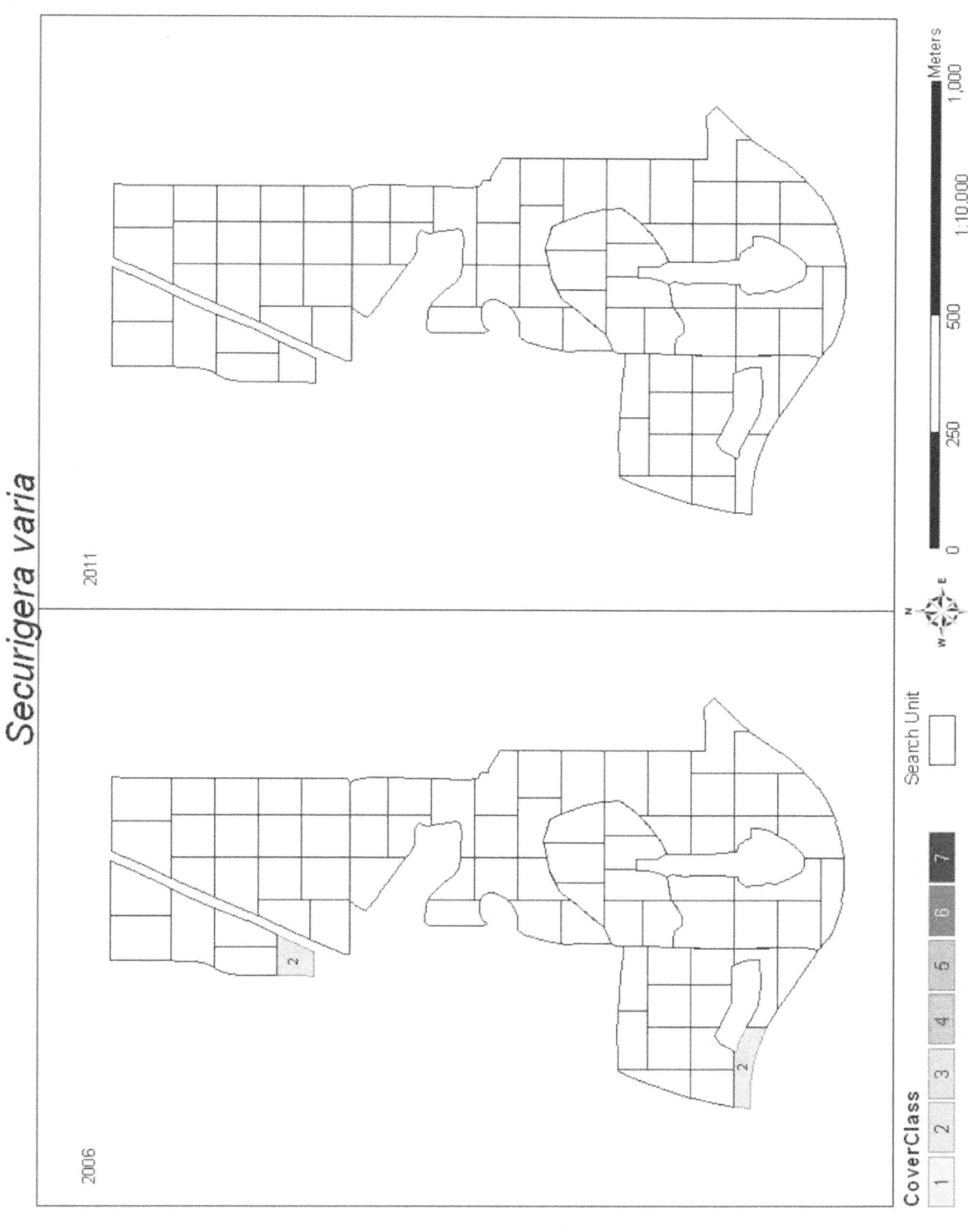

Figure 38. Abundance and distribution of *Securigera varia* (crownvetch) at Lincoln Boyhood National Memorial, 2006 and 2011. Cover classes are as follows: 1=0.1-0.9 m², 2=1-9.9 m², 3=10-49.9 m², 4= 50-99.9 m², 5=100-499.9 m², 6= 500-999.9 m², 7= 1,000-4,999 m².

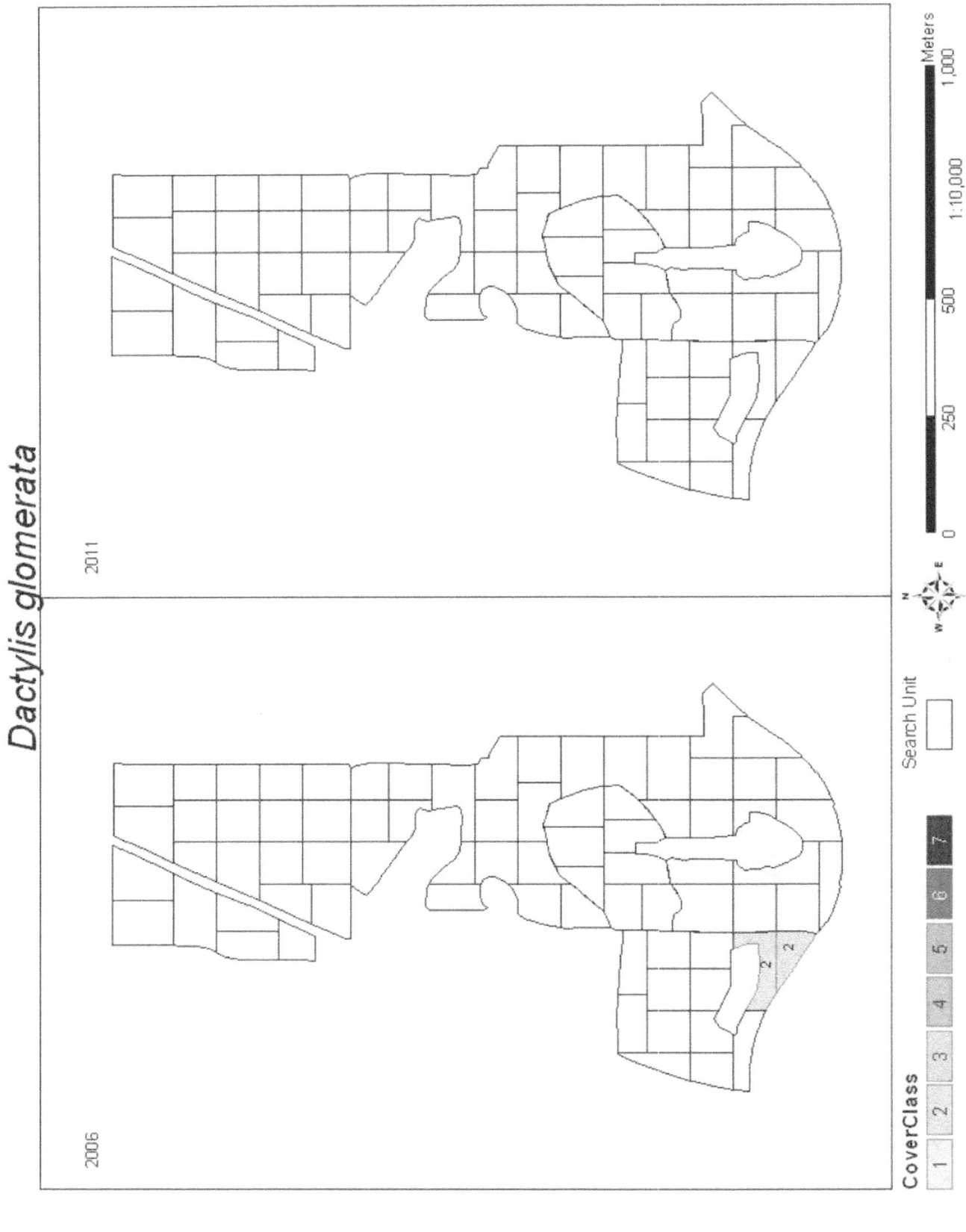

Figure 39. Abundance and distribution of *Dactylis glomerata* (orchardgrass) at Lincoln Boyhood National Memorial, 2006 and 2011. Cover classes are as follows: 1=0.1-0.9 m^2, 2=1-9.9 m^2, 3=10-49.9 m^2, 4= 50-99.9 m^2, 5=100-499.9 m^2, 6= 500-999.9 m^2, 7= 1,000-4,999 m^2.

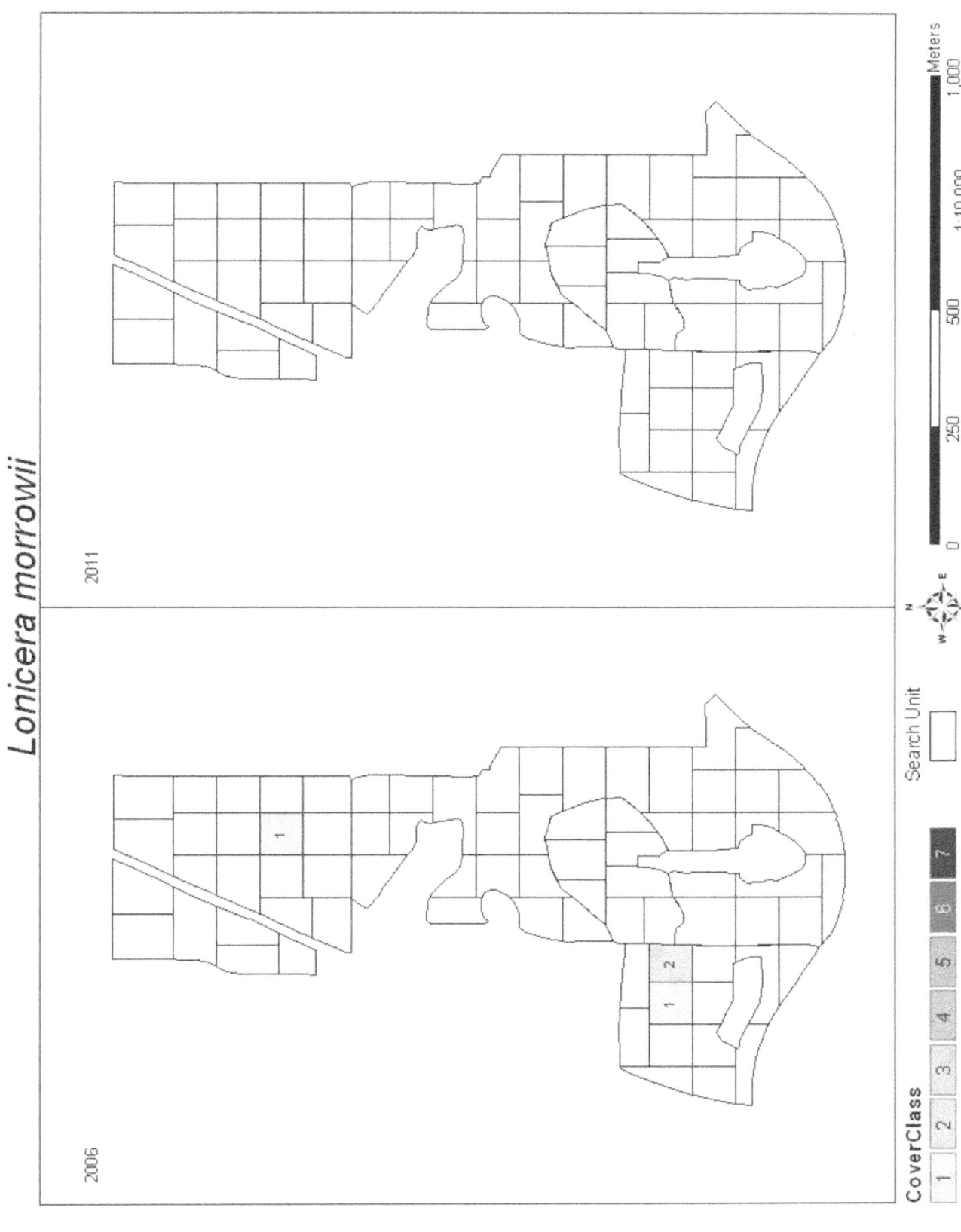

Figure 40. Abundance and distribution of *Lonicera morrowii* (Morrow's honeysuckle) at Lincoln Boyhood National Memorial, 2006 and 2011. Cover classes are as follows: 1=0.1-0.9 m², 2=1-9.9 m², 3=10-49.9 m², 4= 50-99.9 m², 5=100-499.9 m², 6= 500-999.9 m², 7= 1,000-4,999 m².

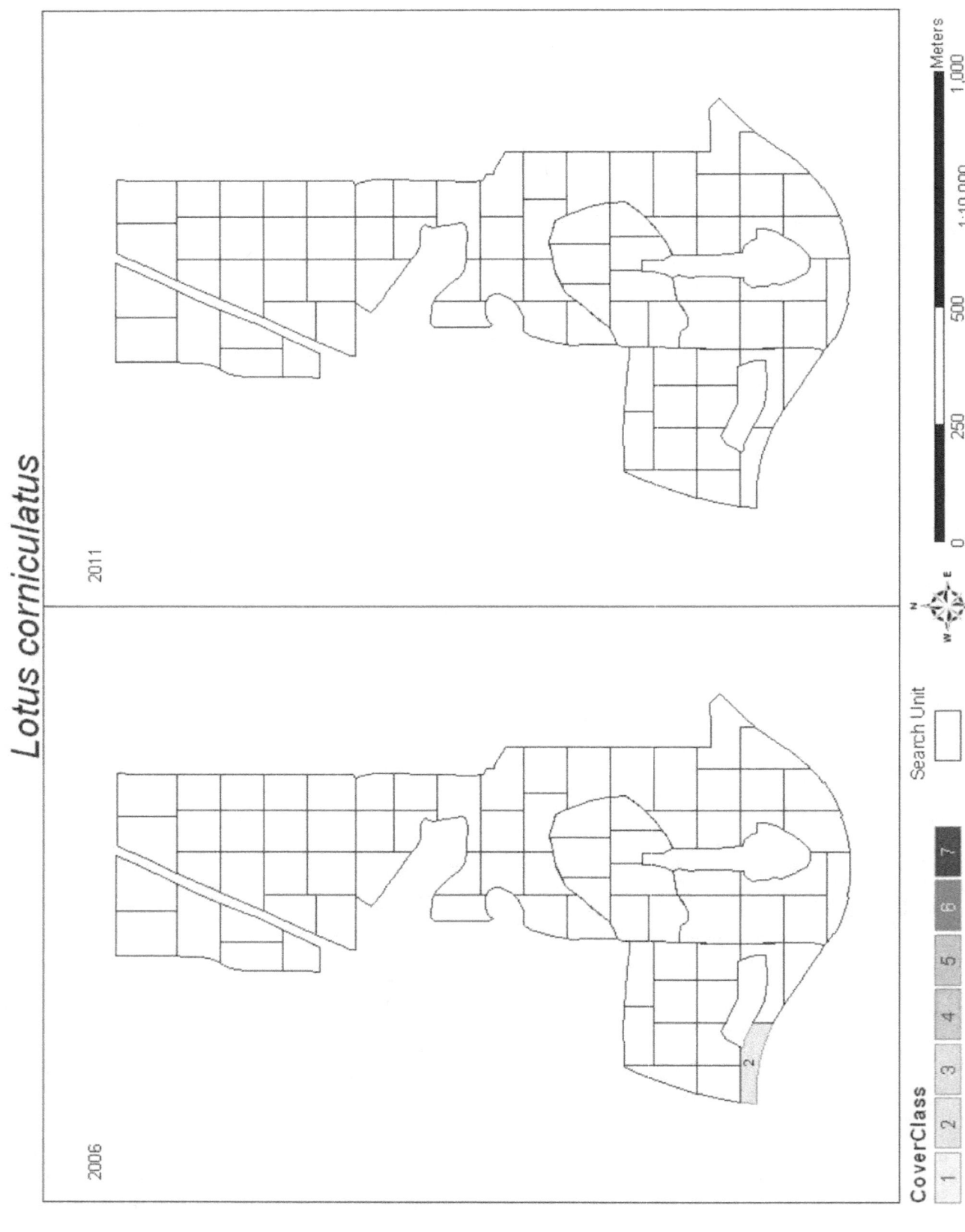

Figure 41. Abundance and distribution of *Lotus corniculatus* (bird's foot trefoil) at Lincoln Boyhood National Memorial, 2006 and 2011. Cover classes are as follows: 1=0.1-0.9 m², 2=1-9.9 m², 3=10-49.9 m², 4= 50-99.9 m², 5=100-499.9 m², 6= 500-999.9 m², 7= 1,000-4,999 m².

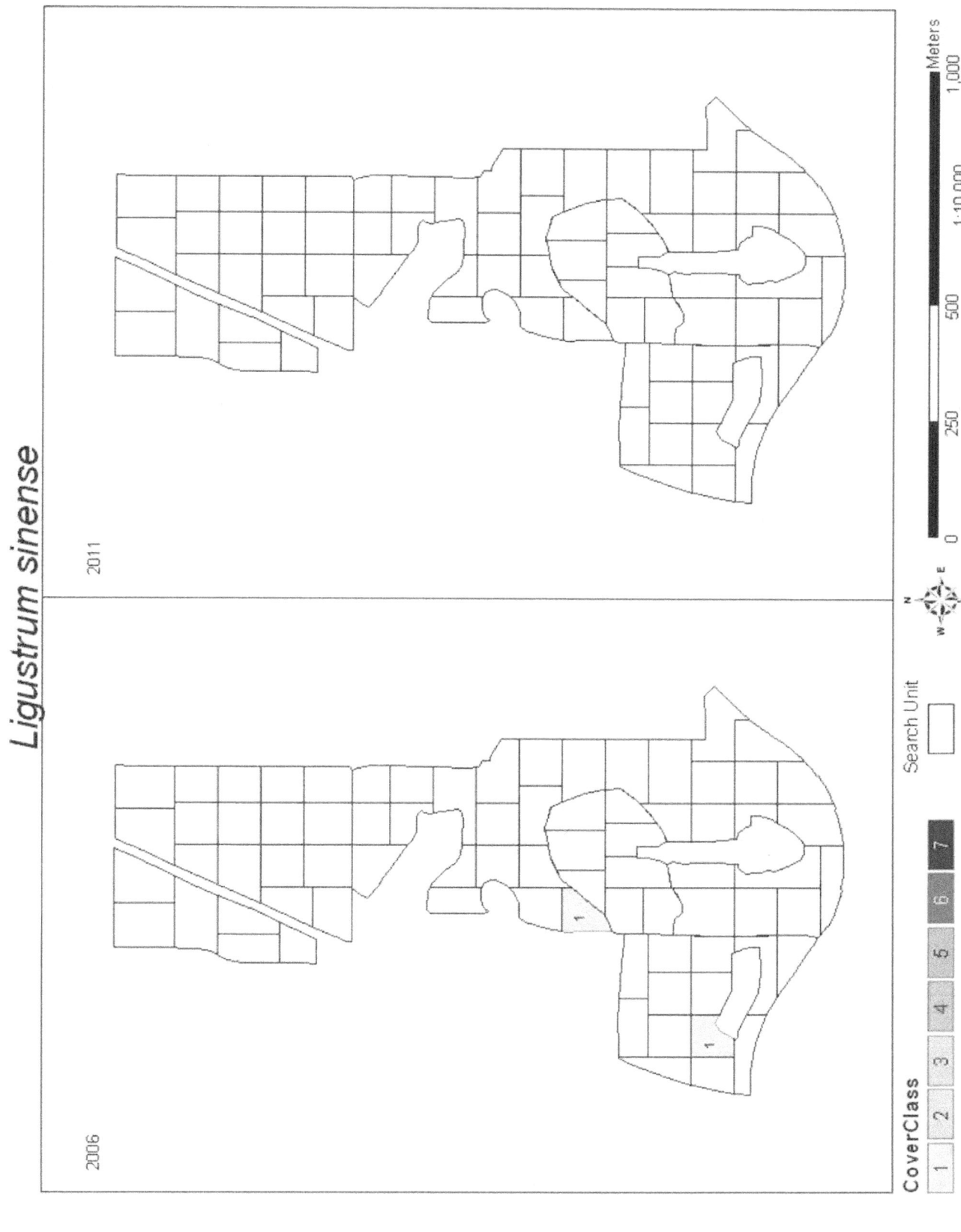

Ligustrum sinense

2011

2006

CoverClass

Search Unit

Figure 42. Abundance and distribution of *Ligustrum sinense* (Chinese privet) at Lincoln Boyhood National Memorial, 2006 and 2011. Cover classes are as follows: 1=0.1-0.9 m^2, 2=1-9.9 m^2, 3=10-49.9 m^2, 4= 50-99.9 m^2, 5=100-499.9 m^2, 6= 500-999.9 m^2, 7= 1,000-4,999 m^2.

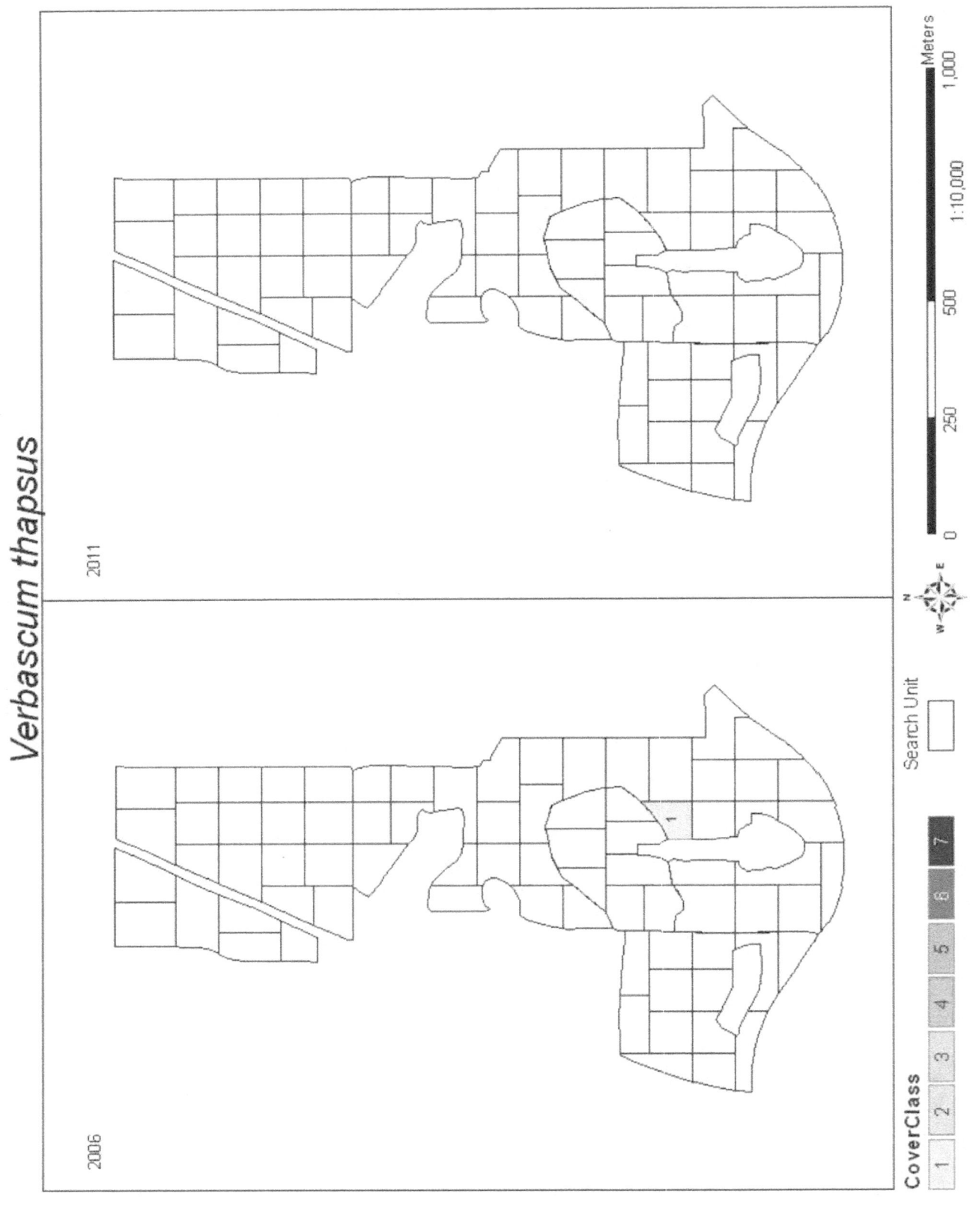

Figure 43. Abundance and distribution of *Verbascum thapsus* (common mullein) at Lincoln Boyhood National Memorial, 2006 and 2011. Cover classes are as follows: 1=0.1-0.9 m², 2=1-9.9 m², 3=10-49.9 m², 4= 50-99.9 m², 5=100-499.9 m², 6= 500-999.9 m², 7= 1,000-4,999 m².

Appendix 1: Invasive Plant Management Scenarios in Cultural Landscapes

Figure 2 summarizes the invasive plant management scenarios that often develop in cultural landscapes. These scenarios are described in greater detail below.

First and foremost, managing invasive plants in cultural landscapes requires preventing unintentional degradation of cultural or natural resources (NPS 2006). This intention is manifest in the Organic Act, establishing the National Park Service, and is further realized within the NPS management policies (2006). Processes outlined under the National Environmental Policy Act and the National Historic Preservation Act structure decision making processes to protect natural and cultural resources while inviting public involvement. Interestingly, invasive plants may be designated as "biotic cultural resources" due to their ethnographic or historic significance (NPS 2006). Typically, however, such plants are incorporated in a recognized cultural landscape, including ethnographic landscapes, historic designed landscapes, historic vernacular landscapes, or historic sites. Managing invasive plants should also not incidentally degrade historic structures or archaeological sites. In rare cases, invasive plants may stabilize archaeological sites, earthworks, or historic buildings. For example, English ivy growing on a historic structure may become integral to the historic fabric and should only be removed based on treatment recommendations found in a historic structures report despite its invasive tendencies. Cultural landscape, ethnographic, and archaeological studies are vital for identifying invasive plants to preserve or control in order to protect cultural and natural resources.

Non-native plant species may also perform certain important functions within parks. Non-native plants may substitute for a closely related native species or be cultivated in areas where native plant alternatives are not suitable to support visitor use or to control erosion (NPS 2006). In these situations, the invasive plant is not a cultural resource nor is it intimately connected to such a resource. The plant may, however, enhance the setting, feeling, or association providing historic context or may serve an important function such as erosion control. The beneficial service that the plant provides in this scenario may be greater than the risk of the plant from spreading beyond the interpretive or historic area. Native species, however, are often available to meet most park needs; consultation with plant materials experts may lead to the identification of appropriate native plants.

After adequately considering cultural resource protection, park resource managers must prioritize invasive plant management needs. Virtually all parks support numerous non-native species; managers are not required to eradicate or control all of these species. Rather managers must determine if control is "prudent and feasible" and if the plant causes one or more of the following impacts (NPS 2006):

1. Interferes with natural processes and the perpetuation of natural features, native species, or natural habitats; or
2. Disrupts the genetic integrity of native species; or
3. Disrupts the accurate presentation of a cultural landscape; or
4. Damages cultural resources; or
5. Significantly hampers the management of park or adjacent lands; or

6. Poses a public health hazard as advised by the U.S. Public Health Service (which includes the Centers for Disease Control and the NPS public health program); or
7. Creates a hazard to public safety.

While these impact criteria provide helpful guidelines in prioritizing invasive plant management actions, the large number of decisions required to move towards specific management approaches and actions in particular parks is often unrecognized.

Invasive plant management treatments that clearly protect earthworks or archeological sites are obvious priorities as described in criterion #4 (see above). Treatments required to protect the historic fabric or integrity of historic buildings or structures also qualify as high priorities. (As stated above, invasive plants may protect resources or provide important historic context and would not be controlled in these cases.) The sensitivity of these resources, however, requires extremely close coordination and planning with cultural resource experts. Consequently, park managers should only conduct these projects after such coordination has occurred.

From a park operations perspective, invasive plants may only be a special case of normal maintenance projects as described in criterion #5 and #7 (see above). Invasive plants, like numerous native species, may threaten visitor safety as hazard trees or as poisonous plants. In agricultural areas within parks, invasive plants may need to be controlled prior to planting. In open fields, invasive plants may be among the woody plant species that require periodic removal in order to hay or mow a site or depict a specific stage of succession. Treatment of invasive plants in these instances happens without explicit consideration of their invasive status. The problem presented by the plant may be amplified, however, because of its ability to reproduce or spread rapidly.

On most parks designated for the protection of historic and cultural resources, invasive plant treatment many be required (as outlined in cultural resource management documents) to maintain a high level of resource integrity. We suspect that the features requiring such attention are generally spatially-restricted in size and include features such as historic horticultural plantings; areas designated as important for education and interpretation; small-patch plant communities or habitats of known biological significance; areas that protect rare, historic, or ethnographically significant plants; and vegetation actively rehabilitated to represent a natural or cultural feature. In accordance with criterion # 1 and #3, invasive plant species should be eradicated or controlled in these areas provided that the resources are not harmed in the process. The limited size of these areas should result in an effort that is usually feasible.

Decisions related to invasive plant management become more complex in areas where cultural landscape features are not designated as contributing features, where active landscape treatments are not required, or where biological significance is negligible. In these situations, vegetation may still contribute to the cultural landscape, and native plant species are typically preferred over non-native species. Within cultural landscape reports, resource professionals may even recommend general conservation goals for these areas such as provision of habitat for wildlife. At this point, managers must consider numerous criteria including:

1. The contribution or potential (short-term or long-term) contribution of the vegetation to the park's designated purpose.

2. Secondary and often more general natural or cultural values associated with the vegetation.
3. Natural processes or management actions affecting the vegetation.
4. Potential spread and impact of particular invasive plant species.
5. Feasibility, in terms of cost, personnel, time commitment, availability of controls, and non-target impacts required for control.

If allowed under a recognized treatment plan, we suggest that park managers first simplify their decisions based solely on the designation of a plant species as invasive and its abundance in the park, which addresses criteria #4 and #5 above. Park managers should determine invasive potential based on scientific literature, gray literature, reported observations within relevant communities of practice, and park management discretion. Abundance may then serve as a proxy for project feasibility as small populations will generally require less time and treatment risks than widespread populations. Eradication from the park is much more likely at this point. In such cases, the time to cover the park searching for the plant is likely the limiting factor. In instances where the entire park cannot be searched, managers may focus on known or suspected geographic areas, physical features such as roads, trails, and streams, or other habitat characteristics that will increase the probability of detection. Despite the expectation of minimized non-target effects, parks must still consider the feasibility of such efforts and potential impacts on park resources.

In the most complex scenario, invasive species are relatively widespread such that eradication is at best a long-term and expensive prospect. The rationale for control in these situations should follow a multi-criteria approach to risk assessment, while inevitably involving a high degree of uncertainty.

Cooperation may increase the "prudence and feasibility" of a project, which may affect the prioritization or the approach taken to manage a particular invasive plant. For example, managers may determine that local efforts cannot successfully control a regionally-established invasive plant species in isolation. If site conditions cannot be changed, re-invasion on the park following treatment would be expected. Cooperative efforts that reduce the probability of re-invasion, however, may elevate the importance of a project. Parks may participate in voluntary cooperative efforts that attempt to control invasive plant species within a larger geographic area. Partnerships between private, non-profit, and government landowners, such as cooperative weed management areas, may organize such initiatives. Cooperative efforts may also be required under state laws. State weed laws, designed primarily to protect agricultural investments, require landowners to control plants that may spread to neighboring properties. As with park-based projects, cooperative efforts that target invasive plant species at an early stage of invasion stand a greater chance for success. Parks must still consider the feasibility of collaborative efforts and potential impacts on park resources.

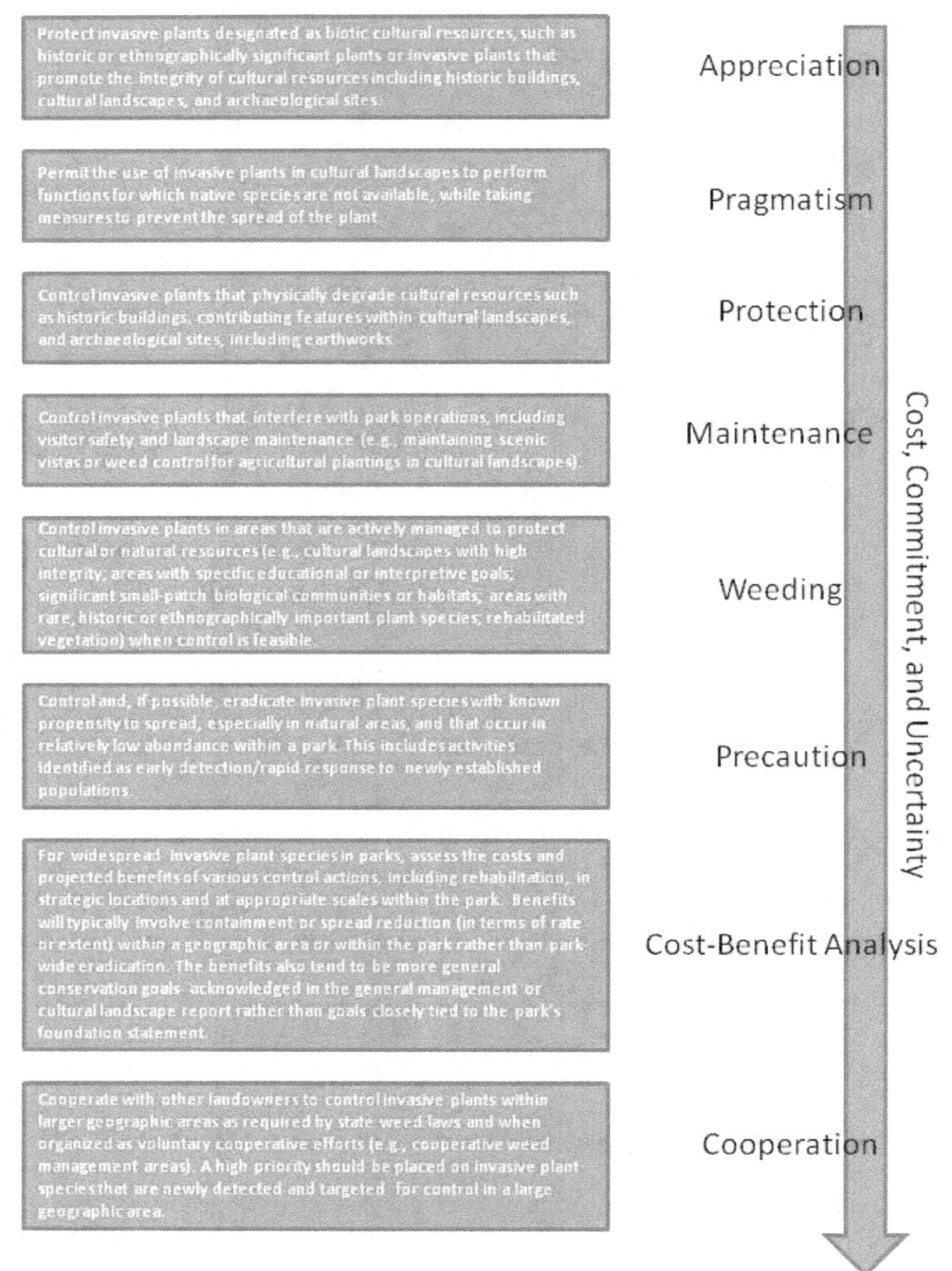

Figure 44. Organization of invasive plant management scenarios applied to cultural landscapes within national park. The scenarios are organized along an axis that generally corresponds with increasing complexity, cost, commitment, and uncertainty associated with the control of a particular invasive plant species. Uncertainty, in this case, refers to uncertainty in the magnitude of the problem caused by an invasive plant as well as uncertainty related to the prospect of control of that plant.

The Department of the Interior protects and manages the nation's natural resources and cultural heritage; provides scientific and other information about those resources; and honors its special responsibilities to American Indians, Alaska Natives, and affiliated Island Communities.

NPS 422/116829, September 2012